No Secrets?

No Secrets?

How Much Honesty Is Good for Your Marriage?

Jeanette C. Lauer & Robert H. Lauer

Zondervan Publishing House
Grand Rapids, Michigan

A Division of **HarperCollins***Publishers*

No Secrets?
Copyright © 1993 by Jeanette C. Lauer, Ph.D.
and Robert H. Lauer, Ph.D.

Requests for information should be addressed to:
Zondervan Publishing House
Grand Rapids, Michigan 49530

Library of Congress Cataloging-in-Publication Data

Lauer, Jeanette C.
   No secrets? : how much honesty is good for your marriage? /
Jeanette and Robert Lauer.
     p. cm.
   ISBN 0-310-37551-7 (paper)
   1. Marriage. 2. Honesty. I. Lauer, Robert H. II. Title.
HQ734.L3362   1993
646.7'8—dc20   93-14383
                                                  CIP

All Scripture quotations, unless otherwise noted, are taken from the HOLY
BIBLE: NEW INTERNATIONAL VERSION®. Copyright © 1973, 1978, 1984
by International Bible Society. Used by permission of Zondervan Publishing House. All rights reserved.

Some of the names in this book have been changed to protect the privacy of
the families described.

Edited by Linda Vanderzalm
Cover design by Ron Kadrmas

Printed in the United States of America

93 94 95 96 97 98 / DH / 10 9 8 7 6 5 4 3 2 1

To our children:
Jon, Kathy, Julie, Jeff, and Kate
and to our grandchildren:
Jeffrey Mathew and Krista Julianne
An honest-to-goodness family

CONTENTS

Introduction   11

1. Honesty Is Never Simple   15
   Honesty Is Complex
   Honesty Is Important
   Building Honest Relationships

PART I
THE MANY SIDES OF DISHONESTY

2. The "Harmless Lie"   27
   Variations on the Theme
   Those Powerful Reasons: Tumbling the
   Walls

3. The Living Contradiction   41
   Contradictions as Destructive
   Variations on the Theme
   Contradictions as a Defense

4. Your Personal Package of Secrets   54
   Your Secret Marital Agreement
   The Hidden-Needs Syndrome
   Attacking the Secrets

5. The Parental Spouse   70
   The Parental Spouse: A Tragedy in Two
   Acts
   One Set of Parents Is Ample
   Variations on the Theme

Parenting Our Spouses
Good-bye Parents, Hello Spouse

6. Family Secrets   86
    The Nature of Family Secrets
    Why Keep the Secret?
    Secret from Whom?
    The Ultimate Example
    What If Someone Finds Out?

PART II

THE HIGH COST OF DISHONESTY

7. The Webs We Weave:
    Seven Things You Can Do
    Without   105
    Loss of Intimacy
    Stunted Growth
    The Web Syndrome
    Diminished Trust
    Unlearned Problem-Solving Skills
    Flawed Witness
    Violating Love

PART III

THE PATTERNS OF HONESTY

8. The Practice of Self-Serving Honesty   121
    Superficial Honesty
    Selective Honesty
    Transparent Honesty

9. The Dangers of Transparent Honesty   133
    Transparent Honesty Hurts
    Many Thoughts and Feelings Are
    Transitory
    Transparent Honesty Can Mask
    Problems

10. The Practice of Loving Honesty   150
    Monitored Honesty
    Change Honesty

PART IV
BUILDING AN HONEST RELATIONSHIP

11. Apples of Gold in the Home   167
    His Talk and Her Talk
    Learning How to Share Feelings
    Learning to Listen

12. Honest-to-Goodness Fighting   183
    The Importance of Conflict
    The Rules of Honest Conflict

13. Speaking the Truth in Love:
    The Bridled Tongue at Work   200
    Why Do I Want to Share This?
    Who Will Benefit?
    With Whom Should I Share This?
    Will It Make Us Feel Closer to Each Other?

14. Allen and Betsy: An Honest Couple   216

INTRODUCTION

*P*eople have called marriage everything from a relationship that makes life complete to an arrangement that inevitably thrusts two people into lives of deception. From the philosophers to the retail clerks, you can hear both high praise and loud groans about the effects of marriage. We've heard both many times. And that's one of the reasons for writing this book. We would like you to be able to talk about marriage with high praise.

For many years we have been experiencing, researching, teaching, writing, and speaking about marriage. People often ask us where we get the ideas for our books and articles. The answer is simple. We get them from talking with hundreds of couples who are struggling to build a fulfilling marriage or to rebuild a marriage that is faltering. We talk with couples in a number of different roles: as researchers, as counselors, as facilitators of marriage-support groups, as leaders of workshops and seminars, and as friends. To some extent, we see in their efforts a reflection of our own quest for a shared life that is both rich and lasting. Our conclusion, after nearly four decades of living and working together, is that the quest is well worth the effort. Marriage can be one of God's greatest blessings in our lives.

This particular book reflects our ongoing effort to

share what we have learned with others. The specific topic grew out of a discussion in a marriage-enrichment group. Dan and Sharon, whose story we tell in the first chapter, started us thinking about the issue of honesty in marriage. We realized that the topic is seldom discussed in any detail. Worse, most people assume honesty is a simple matter; we're either honest or we're not. Everyone knows what it means to be honest. Right?

But from experience we know that the question of honesty is neither simple nor unimportant. As we reflected on the work we had done with couples, we realized that the issue of honesty comes up repeatedly. It comes up in different forms, most of which we explore in this book. However, whatever form it takes, the matter of honesty is crucial to the well-being of a marriage. We agreed that we had to pursue the matter—first in writing an article for *Marriage Partnership* magazine, and then in a more thorough way in this book.

It's important for you to understand the title *No Secrets?* before you read the chapters. First, what do we mean by secrets? You may think of a secret as information that is intentionally withheld from someone else. However, the dictionary indicates that a secret is something that we keep private or something that simply is not apparent. In other words, to say that you have secrets in your marriage is not necessarily to say that either of you is intentionally withholding something from the other. The "secret" may simply be something of which one or both of you are unaware.

For instance, we counseled a couple who accused each other of insensitivity. After listening to the two of them for a while, we noticed a dynamic that neither of them seemed to notice: neither spouse listened to the other. Each was trying so hard to prove a point—that neither ever responded to what the other had said. It was like listening to two monologues interspersed with each other. And when we pointed this out, each looked surprised! The "secret" or "mysterious" malady that had afflicted their marriage was a pattern of speaking without listening to what the other had said.

Second, note that the title is a question. We're raising the question of whether an honest marriage means that the relationship has no secrets. Another way to put it is: Does an honest marriage mean that you never keep anything private? Does it mean that you are always aware of both your thoughts and feelings? The short answer to both questions is no. We'll elaborate on both of these answers in the subsequent chapters.

Finally, we want to point out that all the cases in this book are based on couples with whom we have worked. We have changed names and circumstances to maintain their anonymity. Their experiences, combined with the exercises and principles we offer, should enable you to build an honest marriage that will not only last a lifetime but also enrich you beyond measure.

We are grateful to a number of people who have been important in the development of this book: Ron Lee at *Marriage Partnership*, who not only encourages us but gives us stimulating perspectives; Lyn Cryderman and Sandy Vander Zicht at Zondervan, who gave thumbs up to the project and helped shape it; and the hundreds of couples who have shared something of their married lives with us.

CHAPTER 1

Honesty Is Never Simple

What's the secret of your success?" Usually we pose that question to people who have made a lot of money. We asked it of people who have made lasting and satisfying marriages. It won't surprise you to learn that honesty was one of the important factors. It may surprise you, however, to learn how complicated the subject of honesty in marriage is. "What's there to talk about?" a young man asked when we suggested honesty as a topic for a marriage-support group. "We all know we have to be honest. It's simple."

The question of honesty is definitely *not* a simple matter. On the contrary: what honesty means in a particular situation is often imprecise, and it is always complex. In the following chapters, we will discuss the many dimensions of both honesty and dishonesty. By the end of this book, we hope you will have both a clear idea of what we mean by an "honest marriage" and some clear guidelines on how to achieve it.

HONESTY IS COMPLEX

Let us share with you three examples that illustrate the complexities of honesty. The examples are answers to three questions: Do we always know what is honest and dishonest? Does honesty always help? Does honesty always point us in the right direction?

Do We Always Know What Is Honest?

Do we always know when we're being honest or dishonest? Is the question of honesty at least simple enough that we can easily categorize any particular behavior as either honest or dishonest? Unfortunately the answer is no. In fact, at times we think we are being honest when we're not.

Andrew and Sarah, an engaged couple in their early thirties, came to us for premarital counseling. They took great pride in their honesty with each other. During one of our sessions together, we asked them about their expectations about each other's role in marriage. After an awkward silence Sarah spoke. "After we're married, we'll both be working full time for at least a while. But Andrew has already made it clear that he doesn't intend to do any housework. He'll take care of the outside, but he feels that it's my job to take care of the house."

Andrew remained silent. We pursued the issue. "Sarah, you sound as if you don't agree with that."

"I don't, but—"

Andrew interrupted, "I honestly feel that since I will be bringing in much more money than Sarah, I'm making a larger contribution. So she should take care of the housework. I've always been upfront with Sarah about this."

We suggested, "Perhaps we should talk about this some more. It sounds as if it's already a source of conflict, and it could get more serious after you get married."

Sarah responded, "We've already discussed it a lot. And we get nowhere, so we basically have agreed to disagree."

"That's true. We just have to accept each other's position and let it go at that," Andrew added.

We weren't sure they knew all of their options. "That's one way to handle what seems to be an impasse, but if one of you feels that the situation is an inequitable one, you may be headed for very serious problems. To say you have agreed to disagree sounds as if you have accepted the difference, but, Sarah, you don't appear to be satisfied with the arrangement."

Sarah shifted uncomfortably in her chair. "I'm not, but I just don't know what to do about it so I thought I would try to live with it and see what happens. Andrew and I are so compatible in other ways that I'm hoping this will somehow work out."

It was clear to us that Sarah was not being completely honest, either with herself or with Andrew. She wasn't consciously being dishonest here; she was just confused about what was honest behavior and what was less-than-honest behavior.

In an effort to deal with an issue that seemed impossible to resolve, she had decided to bury her resentment. She hoped the problem would eventually disappear, either by her feelings changing or by Andrew relenting and agreeing to what she considered a more equitable division of labor in the home.

In other words, what she thought was an honest expression of opinion led to an impasse that led to a less-than-honest resolution. Until we discussed the issue with them, Sarah herself was not aware of the extent to which she had slipped out of an honest relationship with Andrew.

Andrew was not blameless in this situation. He wasn't totally honest with Sarah either. As it turned out, Andrew was insecure in his relationship. The fact that he would bring more money into the household was only a rationalization; the real reason he wanted Sarah to agree to do all the housework was his conviction that such behavior would demonstrate her love and commitment to him. He had outwardly accepted the notion that they would "agree to disagree," but he was no more comfortable with that way of resolving the issue than she was.

Each of them pretended to accept something that neither really wanted to accept. And each of them did it for an apparently good reason—to maintain their relationship. Indeed, part of the appeal of dishonesty is that it promises to lead to some good and desired end. But God calls us neither to live out a blunt and insensitive honesty nor to use dishonesty for doing good.

Does Honesty Always Help?

Even if we are not always aware of when we are practicing dishonesty, can we at least say that honesty is simple in the sense that it always helps? Again, the answer is no. It all depends on what you mean by honesty.

Some kinds of honesty can damage a relationship. An incident that took place in one of our marriage-enrichment groups illustrates this possibility. The group was discussing the fact that honesty and openness are vital to a successful relationship. We all agreed that honesty is necessary to create strong bonds between husband and wife and that dishonesty can virtually destroy the intimacy of a Christian union. Just then Sharon, who has been married to Dan for twenty-four years, said that at one point too much honesty nearly wrecked their marriage.

Too much honesty? Is that possible? Isn't complete honesty essential for a fulfilling marriage? After all, even some secular experts say that spouses must be totally transparent with each other, revealing *everything* they think or feel. In this kind of relationship, the couple has no unspoken thoughts, no hidden feelings. Each partner is completely open with the other. But Sharon told us it was precisely Dan's attempt to be totally transparent that caused major difficulties in their marriage.

The problem occurred shortly after Dan had accepted a teaching position at a small midwestern college. This meant they had to move from the large city where they lived to a small town several states away, leaving behind a group of couples who had been their source of support. Unfortunately, the college town they moved into seemed devoid of couples their age. Since Dan's college responsibilities quickly consumed him, Sharon felt lonely and isolated. She recalled the time with a hint of discomfort in her voice. "The only person I talked to all day was our two-year-old son. I suddenly found myself with a totally different life, and I was struggling. I had given up my own work on a master's degree, and I could find no comparable program in the college town. I had to give up my preparation for my own future career temporarily. But Dan was riding high. He loved his work, and he got lots of attention. The young female students were attracted to him. And worse, he was attracted to one of them. He was in his 'honesty' phase and decided to tell me all about it."

Sharon had a pained look on her face. Even after fifteen years, it was clear that it still hurt her to talk about the experience. "Well, I was just devastated," she said. "I felt that not only had my life been radically changed by the move, but now my marriage was threatened as well."

Dan's feelings for his student did not last long. And his behavior never went beyond flirtation. He loved Sharon and remained true to his commitment to her. Yet at the time, his revelation created a crisis in their relationship. He insisted that he had told her only because he wanted to be totally honest in order to maintain their intimacy. However, for Sharon, his disclosure meant a shattering of that intimacy for a time.

We must admit that Dan was being honest. But Sharon's reaction raises a lot of questions. Did Dan talk too freely about his feelings? Did Dan reveal his feelings for the sake of their marriage or for his own needs? And if his confession reflected his own needs, was Sharon the best person to whom to confess, or would he have been wiser to talk to someone else?

Eventually, they worked through the problem. But, as Dan told our marriage-enrichment group, sharing his feelings in the expectation that it would make his marriage a "truly honest" relationship backfired. It took time for them to recapture their former level of intimacy and for Sharon to trust Dan fully around other women.

"At that point in my life," Sharon concluded, "honesty wasn't what I needed. I needed support and understanding and reassurance. Dan's so-called honesty really hurt our marriage for a while."

Does Honesty Clearly Point the Way?

We've seen so far that honesty is complex: We're not always aware when we're being dishonest, and we can't be sure that honesty will be helpful in every situation. But we *can* know one thing for sure—what it means to be honest or dishonest in a particular situation. Right? One final time, the answer is no. The quality of honesty is not a guide that gives clear directions on how to behave.

We can be honest in a variety of ways in the same situation. For example, consider the old saying: You can make a fool of yourself without even knowing it—unless, of course, you're married. Although the saying is satirical, it underscores one of the things spouses do for each other: help each other be aware of inappropriate public behavior. To make a spouse aware of inappropriate behavior is to be honest with him or her. But how do you do that? Do you simply say, "You really made a fool of yourself tonight," or "I was so embarrassed by the way you acted tonight that I could have died on the spot"? Both statements are an honest expression of what you're feeling, but are they the best way to approach the problem?

Marriage counselors frequently hear discussions like the following. How would you rate each in terms of reflecting an honest relationship?

> **She:** "He always makes derogatory remarks about my cooking."

He: "Well, she really can't cook very well. That's just the simple truth."

He: "She gives the cat more affection than she gives me."

She: "I have a hard time expressing affection. He knew that when he married me. He should tell me what he needs."

He: "Everybody needs affection. She should know that."

She: "I get angry at him for something, and then I get even angrier because he won't confront the problem with me."

He: "I believe a lot of things aren't worth fighting about. Why not just forget it and let it go away?"

She: "But you don't really forget. You stew about it. It doesn't go away because we never resolve it."

He: "That's because you can't let it go."

In each of these interchanges, the speakers are honest with each other about how they feel. But the way in which they are expressing their honest feelings is not necessarily conducive to building marital intimacy.

Our point is that even if we agree that it's important to be honest, we have not yet settled the matter of just how we go about being honest in a constructive, much less, Christian manner. We can be literally honest in many different ways in a particular situation. For instance, at the Last Supper, the disciples had a dispute "as to which of them was considered to be greatest" (Luke 22:24). Jesus needed to be honest with them about their pettiness and self-serving thinking. He dramatized what discipleship should be by washing their feet.

Think of the other ways in which Jesus could have been honest about their behavior. He could have, for instance, verbally rebuked their self-centeredness. He could have condemned their blindness in the face of his own example of humility. He could have angrily pointed out their insensitivity at a time when he stood in the shadow of the Cross. He could have walked away from them and grieved about their spiritual poverty. These and other methods all would honestly depict the character of the wrangling disciples on that night. But none of these methods would have affected them as dramatically as the foot washing did.

Jesus knew that the method we use to express honest thoughts and feelings is as important as the honesty itself.

In summary, honesty in marriage and family life is a complex topic. As the story of Dan and Sharon well illustrates, we frequently face a dilemma rather than a simple choice of doing "the Christian thing." The question is not *whether* to be honest; the question is *how* to be honest.

HONESTY IS IMPORTANT

What exactly is honesty? The word is not found in the New Testament. The Greek words that are translated as "honest" or "honesty" in some versions mean such things as good, blameless, holy, and worthy of respect.

But the fact that the Bible doesn't specifically tell us to be honest doesn't mean the notion is not a Christian one. Honesty refers to such things as uprightness, truthfulness, candor, integrity, and being free from deceit. Jesus praised honesty when he called Nathanael a man "in whom there is nothing false" (John 1:47). Peter called us to honesty when he admonished us to rid ourselves of deceit (1 Peter 2:1).

The importance of honesty in marriage relationships is seen both in the damage to a marriage marred by dishonesty (discussed in chapter 7) and in the benefits that honesty brings to marriage (discussed in the last part of this book). We have seen long-term, happy marriages deteriorate rapidly when one of the partners discovered that the other had been consistently dishonest about some aspect of their relationship. And we have seen other marriages that have weathered all kinds of assaults because the couple had maintained an honest relationship with each other throughout their marriage.

In other words, honesty in our intimate relationships is not a minor topic. The lack of honesty imperils marriage by undercutting one of the main pinions—the ability to trust each other. Whatever else, we need to be able to trust our spouses. We need to have confidence that those we love will not knowingly betray, deceive, abandon, or neglect us. Only then can we have the kind of marriage that God intended for us, the kind that enriches and sustains us throughout our lives.

BUILDING HONEST RELATIONSHIPS

The call to honesty is also a challenge to our faith. We can see this challenge in the following questions.

- How can you be honest without being blunt and insensitive?
- How can you maintain your integrity as a Christian spouse and avoid inflicting the kind of pain that Dan gave to Sharon?
- What do you do when truthfulness and love seem to clash in a particular situation?
- Is it deceitful to withhold something even though your spouse hasn't asked you about it?
- Does honesty mean that you become an "open book" to your spouse?

As we address such questions in subsequent chapters, we will ground our discussion in biblical principles. We will also draw on our experiences with the numerous couples with whom we have worked both in counseling and in marriage enrichment. And we will focus on this goal: to provide you with some tools for building an honest marriage so that you may have both an enduring and a fulfilling experience of intimacy in your relationship.

Note that we say *both* enduring and fulfilling. Virtually

every Christian who stands in the presence of God and takes the marriage vows intends for the union to last. Virtually every Christian who enters marriage intends to build a stable home life for both the spouse and the children. Nevertheless, the chances of disruption, even for Christians, are uncomfortably high.

On the other hand, just because a marriage lasts doesn't mean that it's the fulfilling kind of union that God intends for us to have. We did a study of 351 couples who have been married for fifteen or more years to identify the factors that kept them together. We found that, in spite of their long marriages, nearly fifteen percent of the couples experienced unhappiness for one or both spouses. Among those couples, the marriage had lasted either "for the children's sake" or because of religious convictions against divorce. But the marriage lacked the richness and vitality of a satisfying union.

To have your marriage not only last but also be fulfilling, you will need to nurture the quality of honesty. You will need to understand the sometimes subtle ways in which a relationship can slip into dishonesty as well as the loving ways in which you can pursue honesty. We hope this book will help you do that.

Part I
The Many Sides of Dishonesty

Do not deceive one another.
LEVITICUS 19:11

CHAPTER 2

The "Harmless Lie"

What is a "harmless lie"? Presumably, it is a statement that is technically not the truth, but because it's not a blatant, overt lie, we believe it to be harmless. Our intentions are good, we claim. We want to spare someone's feelings or safeguard our relationship with that person. Thus, we justify harmless lies by saying such things as: "I didn't want to hurt his feelings"; "What she doesn't know won't hurt her"; and "I didn't really have another engagement, but it was the only way I could get out of going without hurting her feelings."

We can see the harmless lie in action in the story of Jacob and Laban. Jacob offered to work seven years in order to marry Laban's younger daughter, Rachel. Laban replied, "It's better that I give her to you than to some other man. Stay here with me" (Gen. 29:19). Apparently Laban agreed to Jacob's offer. But carefully read what Laban said. Technically, Laban never told Jacob that he would give Rachel to him after seven years, even though Jacob believed that's what he had said. Seven years later, Jacob discovered that in the darkness of night he had married Leah instead of Rachel. He asked why Laban had deceived him so.

Think about the various ways in which Laban could justify his harmless lie. One is the justification he made to Jacob: "It is not our custom here to give the younger daughter in marriage before the older one" (Gen. 29:26). He might also have told himself that in the long run Jacob would realize that he had gained two good wives instead of one. Or that in any case he had acted in a way that was necessary for Leah's well-being.

The way we justify harmless lies is the same way that Laban did: we say they are sometimes unavoidable in order to do what is necessary and right. But the deception probably contributed to the strained relationship between Jacob and Laban in subsequent years. Deception and intimacy, like oil and water, simply don't mix.

VARIATIONS ON THE THEME

The problem with the harmless lie is that it can so easily become a pattern rather than an isolated incident. The pattern can take various forms, all of which threaten the integrity of intimate relationships.

The Word Craftsman

Like Laban, some people are what we call word craftsmen, those who are skilled in phrasing things so that they always technically tell the truth even while they deceive others. Laban could have said to Jacob, "I never promised to give you Rachel after seven years. I just said it would be better for you than someone else to marry her. And I told you to stay with me." Laban's words skillfully led Jacob to believe something that Laban never promised.

Sometimes others help word craftsmen in their task. Near a university in which we once taught was a bar named "The Library." By the owner's choice of names, he enabled a number of the students who were budding word craftsmen to tell their parents that they had spent an afternoon at "the library." The parents were no doubt delighted at what they believed to be the studious habits of their children, and the children were delighted at the opportunity to indulge themselves while doing what they believed to be no harm to their parents.

Nevertheless, deceit is no less wrong and no less damaging to intimacy simply because the words themselves are literally true. Beverly, a young homemaker, and her husband, Phil, an accountant, had to come to counseling after she discovered she was married to a word craftsman. She was distraught, "Phil is a fine Christian man, and I know this doesn't sound like a big deal to some people, but it really bothers me that he isn't always honest about how he feels. He says he never lies to me, and I guess that's true as far as what he says. But it's still dishonest because he leads me to think he feels a certain way, and then I find out that it isn't true."

As an example, Beverly told about the time when she had asked Phil if he minded going to her sister's home for part of their vacation: "I knew that Phil preferred for us to be by ourselves on vacation, but I don't have any other time to see my sister. And I just wanted to spend a part of the vacation there, not the whole thing. I thought that was okay with him. When we got there, I could tell he was unhappy about it. We got into an argument soon after we arrived. I pointed out that he had told me that he didn't mind going. He insisted he never said that. However, that's sure the impression he gave me."

What exactly had Phil said? They don't each remember the same thing, but it was something like, "We can go there if you need to spend that time with your sister." Beverly assumed that meant he didn't mind.

"But I didn't say I didn't mind," Phil protested.

Beverly's voice rose in anger. "That's just the problem. I would rather you tell me just how you feel in the first place. Then we can figure out what to do. Instead, you always give me misleading answers. I don't think that I should have to analyze everything you say to figure out if you're telling me the whole truth."

What is truth? Clearly, it is something more than crafting together words that are literally true. The person who carefully crafts words may not be telling an overt lie, but neither is he or she engaged in an honest relationship.

People who craft their words carefully to avoid the truth have various reasons for their behavior, and some think they are following the best or the only acceptable way. Yet in every instance of deceit, we can find an alternative that is both honest and conducive to a healthy relationship. In the case of Beverly and Phil, for example, both had to change their behavior. Beverly thought the fault was entirely Phil's. But she contributed to the problem by too quickly assuming that what she wanted to hear was what Phil had said. Beverly had to learn to listen carefully and keep the conversation going until she was sure what Phil was saying.

Phil, on the other hand, had a harder change to make. He had learned as a child to mask his feelings with verbal craftsmanship. His parents had been harsh disciplinarians; early on he had learned how to mollify them without technically lying. He now had to work on expressing his true feelings and taking the risk that sometimes Beverly would not like the way he truly felt. They would have some short-term difficulties, we told them. But as they increased their skills in listening and disclosing, they would build a rich marriage that would otherwise certainly elude them.

The Secret-Compartment Marriage

Jan and David seem to have a strong marriage now. We're not sure of the long-term prospects, however. We discovered something that David doesn't know: Jan has a secret compartment in their relationship, an activity that she consistently hides from David. It isn't anything dramatic. It's simply that she hides her department-store purchases from David. She is able to do that because she writes the checks for the household expenses each month. David is confident of Jan's ability to take care of their finances; thus he never bothers to check on the status of their accounts. Moreover, he doesn't notice what she wears, so he never questions whether an outfit is new.

Why does Jan maintain this secret part of her life? Early in their marriage, Jan and David had jointly handled the family's finances and paid the monthly bills together. David had regularly balked at the department-store charges and complained about how much Jan spent on clothing. For a while, she curtailed her purchases. But when David's professional responsibilities increased, Jan volunteered to take over the bill-paying chore; unfortunately, she also resumed her old pattern of shopping.

Jan freely shared her secret with us. She is not embarrassed by it because she sees it as her only option. She doesn't feel she's lying because David never asks her about the matter. Moreover, the money she spends is not simply self-indulgence. As a professional woman, she needs a good wardrobe. As a wife, she doesn't want constant bickering about the amount she spends on clothes. "So, the bottom line," she told us, "is that I'm being a proper professional and a good wife, and no harm is done."

Jan has a quiver full of sharp reasons with which she can shoot down any objection to her behavior. But what happens if David finds out what she has been doing? What happens if she decides that she wants to keep another area of their relationship secret? How fulfilling can a marriage be if you feel compelled consistently to hide something from your spouse? And how does that behavior square with Christian integrity?

Jan, like all the moral descendants of Laban, feels that she has no other option. She is simply doing what she has to do under the circumstances.

But we can always find better options. We would suggest that Jan choose a time when both she and David are relaxed and not weary from work and ask him to discuss her clothing needs. She could tell him what she has been doing, tell him that she is sorry for deceiving him, and stress the point that she has made her purchases out of a sense of professional need. She could then ask him to talk with her until they come to some agreement about her needs so that she doesn't have to hide her purchases any more.

In the process, Jan would have to be flexible about those needs (it's not clear that she needs all that she buys). But what if David refuses to compromise even if Jan is willing to do so? We doubt that would happen, but if it came to that, we would suggest that Jan say: "I'm sorry you feel that way. I had hoped we could agree. Since you won't budge, I'm going to have to buy the clothes I need anyway. I won't try to hide the amount I spend from you. I'm going to be honest with you from now on because I think that's important for our marriage. I know you won't like the amount I spend, and I regret that. For the time being, I guess we'll just have to each live with a situation that neither of us is happy about. But in any case, I want us to have an honest relationship even if we can't agree on this issue."

Jan and David's situation illustrates that a secret compartment may involve no overt lie. Furthermore, the intent may be good—to preserve harmony in the relationship. Another example is Fran, a thirty-five-year-old homemaker, who has what she calls a "benevolent sugar bowl"—her secret stash of money, saved out of her household allowance. She uses it to make small purchases, "those important little extras," for herself and her children.

Her husband doesn't know about the sugar bowl, but Fran makes the point that she is simply using money that is given to her for family needs in a way that she finds pleasing. She agrees that if her husband knew, he would want to put the leftover money into savings. Rather than work the issue out and risk arguing about it, she has chosen to keep her secret compartment. It is, she insists, harmless to her husband and beneficial to her and the children.

But both Fran and her husband lose something in this situation. The sugar bowl is not merely harmless to him or benevolent for her. Commitment is neither a part-time nor a contingent decision. Marriage is not a matter of saying to someone, "I will become one flesh with you, in every way except . . ." To hide systematically some aspect of your life from your spouse both violates the biblical ideal of marriage and detracts from the quality of your intimacy. Fran's husband may never miss the money, but they will both miss the full richness of an honest marriage.

The Other-Life Spouse

Is it possible for someone to have a whole other life that one's spouse knows nothing about? Consider Mae, who has been married for nearly forty years to Ben, a retired merchant. On the surface, it seems to be a good marriage. They have stayed together, and they rarely have the kind of heated arguments they had in their earlier years. Yet they have always felt a certain tension in their relationship, a tension that we believe is rooted in Mae's "other life."

In this case, the other life is actually one of Christian caring. Mae believes in helping those in need; Ben believes that "God helps those who help themselves." Mae believes that Christians should spend time with those who are suffering; Ben believes it's not good to interfere in other people's business.

Ben and Mae ran a small grocery store throughout most of their working lives. We first became acquainted with Mae's other life when she asked us to take a basket of groceries to a needy family at Thanksgiving time. We thought she might like the joy of taking them herself. "Oh no," she said, "I can't. Ben mustn't find out."

Somewhat startled, we made the delivery. Gradually we found out about Mae's other life. She would visit relatives when Ben went fishing. She sent money to people she knew were in need, but always in cash and always in secret. She helped a niece whose husband was unemployed by sending her groceries, but never with Ben's knowledge. Since they retired from business, she spends much time shopping for her daughter-in-law, but Ben knows nothing of the purchases she makes.

Mae has enjoyed her good deeds. However, she has always felt tense about them because Ben might somehow discover what she is doing. And like the others we have discussed, Mae is certain that she has no alternative if she is to continue helping others: "What I do doesn't keep Ben from doing anything he wants. And it doesn't keep him from buying anything he needs. But I know he wouldn't allow me to keep on doing what I want to do if he knew about it. He's a good husband, but he doesn't believe much in charity."

Mae should have addressed the problem at the beginning of her marriage. What would have happened if she had told Ben that, as a Christian, she had certain responsibilities to care for others? We don't know. But certainly nothing worse than the forty years of secrecy and tension she has endured with him.

Mae chose her other life. Some spouses have another life by default. This happens when both are so immersed in careers or other responsibilities that a large segment of each of their lives is hidden from the other, and for the most part, they maintain separate lives. We're not talking here about couples who both work and each of whom has some interests, hobbies, and friends separate from the other. To some extent, that describes most couples. Rather, we are talking about couples whose lives seldom seem to coincide, who seem more like "two ships passing in the night" than husband and wife. Is that dishonest? It is in the sense that the ideal for marriage is that the couple becomes "one flesh." That ideal is impossible when a significant portion of one or both spouses' lives is hidden.

A pizzeria near our home advertises itself as offering an "honest pizza." The point they're making is that they make a pizza the way it's supposed to be made—with real cheese, among other things.

For Christians, then, an honest marriage is one that becomes what it is supposed to be—a true union of two people. And that simply can't be done when one or both spouses have a completely separate other life, even if the other life is by default rather than by design.

Consider Travis and Jane. They've been married four years but still feel as if they have barely begun to have a real marriage. As Travis put it, "Jane and I both work, and we both work long hours. Unfortunately, we also sometimes work different hours. So about the only time we really have together is on the weekends. It's almost as if we have to get reacquainted every weekend. And by the time we begin to feel comfortable with each other again, it's back to the rat race."

Jane agreed. "It's as if we can't get beyond a certain point because we never have the time. It takes the whole weekend just to catch up on what we've each been doing during the past week. I'd love to have time with Travis just to sit and talk about some of the things he's feeling, where we're headed in our marriage, and what he hopes to achieve. I'd love to talk more with him about his experiences growing up and tell him about mine."

Jane groped for the words to express exactly how she felt. Then her face brightened with understanding: "The weekend barely allows us to take care of the essentials. But we have no time at all for the luxuries of intimacy. And I'm not sure either one of us is going to be content in the long run without some of those luxuries."

Many two-career couples are experiencing the kind of frustration Jane and Travis feel. We once asked the marriage-enrichment group at our church to keep a record of their conversations during the week. At the next meeting, we would use their records as a basis for talking about communication in marriage. The following week the husband in one of the two-career marriages ruefully noted, "We were appalled at how little we communicate during the week. We realize now that we have to get a whole week's worth of communication into a couple of days. The only time we really talk in any depth at all is on the weekend. And even then, one of us occasionally has to go into work."

Such couples, of course, are working hard and trying

to live as respectable, self-supporting people. Is it fair to say that their marriage falls short of Christian honesty?

Some will not think it fair, but we believe it is a fair assessment. We repeat: As long as a significant portion of your life is hidden from your spouse—whether by design or default—you fall short of an honest marriage in which you are becoming one flesh.

Does this mean that two-career couples can't have an honest Christian marriage? Not at all. As with other variations, there are always alternatives, ways to increase the amount of sharing. For example, we know some couples who make a point of calling each other at work. They may exchange little more than a short "love message" on occasion, but they at least have some daily time that otherwise would be lost.

We know a minister whose wife is a nurse. She works days, and he works days as well as many nights. One way they increase their time together is to meet for dinner somewhere on the nights when he has to return to church for a meeting. They also both rise early in the morning to spend some time together, and they call each other during the day.

Couples can find many ways to avoid having one or both of them develop another life that is unknown to the other. And if you feel that isn't possible, then you must make a choice. Jesus made it clear that we often come face to face with such choices. We can't serve two masters (Matt. 6:24). If spouses truly can find no way to nurture their intimacy in the face of career demands, then they face the choice of continuing those particular careers at the expense of their relationship or finding other careers that allow time to build an honest marriage. When faced with such a choice, we need to remember the saying: "No one says, at the end of life, 'I wish I had spent more time at the office.'"

THOSE POWERFUL REASONS: TUMBLING THE WALLS

Why do Christians get caught up in maintaining a dishonest marriage? As we have seen, their reasons seem *so* right, and they make the deception seem *so* necessary. The reasons become walls that shut out any efforts to alter the situation. Let's look more closely at those walls in an attempt to bring the walls tumbling down.

The Wall of Harmlessness

On the surface, harmless lies frequently appear to be justified. In Jan and David's situation, for example, what if David never finds out about Jan's department-store purchases? He hasn't, after all, for five years. Won't her deception then prove to be harmless?

Of course, by "harmless" Jan means that David isn't hurt. And she certainly doesn't feel hurt herself; in fact, she feels that she is helping herself. But "harm" has many facets. People like Jan are hurting themselves, their spouses, and other people in a number of ways:

- They deprive their spouses and themselves of the richness of a fully honest relationship.
- They diminish their intimacy by systematically hiding an aspect of their lives.
- They provide a flawed model of marriage for their children and for young Christians generally.
- They add to the sum total of deceit and dishonesty that pervades and corrupts our society.
- They compromise their own integrity as Christians.

In the light of such consequences, we do not believe it's possible to argue that the kind of "harmless lies" we have discussed can ever be said to be harmless.

The Wall of Maintaining Harmony

A number of the spouses we have discussed in this chapter pointed out that the attempt to be honest would bring about serious conflict in their marriages. Surely, maintaining harmony is important, isn't it?

Maintaining harmony in your marriage should never be the highest priority. In fact, some horrendous things have happened in families where one member tried to maintain or restore harmony at all costs. For instance, consider the story of Becky, a young woman struggling to be a useful Christian. Becky is fighting her past; she said that she is still overwhelmed by feelings as she shared her story with us. Becky was a victim of incest in a strife-torn home: "My home was always a tense place. My parents often had volatile arguments that frightened me terribly. Even now, a raised voice causes me to freeze until laughter accompanies it. No one I knew could effectively stand up to my father. My mother took the brunt of his wrath, and I was extremely protective of her."

Like many victims of incest, Becky had, until recently, blocked a good deal of the experience out of her mind. So she isn't sure exactly when it began, but she thinks she was about eleven when her father first violated her. Why didn't she resist? You have to understand what it meant to her. She says: "I didn't react to the incest as a sexual act but as a way to keep the family together. I know now how much I felt responsible for my parents' feelings and well-being. I desperately wanted harmony in my family, and every other need became subordinate to that. I saw myself as the buffer between my parents and the protector of my brothers and sisters as well as my mother when my father was hurting her. And I could not imagine having behaved otherwise."

Becky's story underscores the fact that, while harmony in the home is a Christian ideal, we should not always pursue peace at any cost. The price of Becky's silence was extreme personal pain and the perpetuation of a disastrous family situation. Most importantly, it wasn't until Becky told the truth about her situation that the healing could begin for her and her family.

In most cases, the cost of being honest does not permanently impair harmony. Rather it usually requires a relatively brief time for working out a compromise. Unfortunately, for many of us, working out a compromise is one of those hassles that we would rather avoid. However, the gain in marital satisfaction is immense and well worth the hassle.

The Wall of Necessity

Perhaps necessity—the argument that there is no alternative—is one of the more imposing of the walls that help maintain deceit in marriage. However, we have already shown that we can always find alternatives, even if the alternative means that one or both of you have to compromise your preferences.

Compromise is something that virtually everyone agrees with in principle but few of us like in practice. The dislike stems from a feeling that the net result is something less than the best for either person. That point of view was expressed by a wife with whom we counseled. As we talked about compromise, she looked glum. "The problem with compromise is that you both lose. It's as if I want a red house and he wants a white house, so we buy a pink house. And we both lose."

Our response was, "You both lose only if the color of the house is more important than your relationship. But if your relationship is more important than the color of the house, then you both have won. Because you have maintained what is most important—your marriage."

We believe that the wall of necessity comes tumbling down in the face of this kind of reasoning. That is, honesty may force you to confront an issue and work toward some kind of compromise. You shouldn't think of the compromise as a lose-lose situation or even as a less-than-best situation.

You have made a marriage commitment that gives your
relationship priority over anything else except your commitment to God. Whatever you do to maintain and enrich that
relationship is not a loss but a gain.

CHAPTER 3

The Living Contradiction

*R*ay, an engineering draftsman, has been married to Jean, a medical technician, for ten years. They have two children and a fairly satisfying marriage. We say "fairly" because Jean is troubled by one aspect of their relationship. "Ray sometimes gets stressed out from his work, or he feels down about something. I know when something is bothering him, but I never am sure what it is. It could be me, for all I know, because when I ask him about it, I always get the same reply. He insists that nothing is wrong."

Ray responded, "But what if it's true that nothing's the matter?"

Jean was quick to retort, "You may say that nothing is the matter, but your face and body tell me that something is really bothering you. I believe what I see and not what I hear. And you have to agree that if I really work at it and insist that you tell me, you'll finally admit that something is wrong and tell me what it is."

Ray grudgingly acknowledged that it was difficult for him to talk about his feelings when something upset or bothered him. He didn't want Jean to notice or say anything because "it will pass sooner or later, and I'll be all right."

Jean was not satisfied with that, however. "But what if it's *me* that you're upset with?" she asked. "I can't wait until you feel better and just hope that it's something else. Besides," she added, "I can help you. Aren't we supposed to do that for each other?"

Ray is just one example of what we call the "living contradiction." In his case, the contradiction was between what he said and the way he looked. Jean had lived with him long enough to trust his looks rather than his words. She finally had reached the point, however, where she was weary of trying to force him to talk about what was bothering him.

In order to rescue their marriage from deterioration, Ray needs to work on learning to express his feelings to his wife. When something bothers him, Jean needs to know whether he is troubled by something in their relationship or something else. If he learns to talk about his feelings, they both, along with their relationship, will benefit.

CONTRADICTIONS AS DESTRUCTIVE

The living contradiction—pretending to be one thing while acting in a way that contradicts it—is destructive in a number of ways. Consider several biblical examples. Joab was a living contradiction in his dealings with Amasa (2 Sam. 20). King David, in an effort to unite his kingdom, had removed Joab as commander of his army and replaced him with Amasa. But the Israelites continued their rebellious ways. When a Benjamite named Sheba led a new rebellion against David, he sent Amasa on a three-day mission to mobilize the men of Judah. When Amasa did not return in three days, David sent out his army under the command of Abishai to attack Sheba. Along the way, they met Amasa. Joab greeted Amasa: "'How are you, my brother?' Then Joab took Amasa by the beard with his right hand to kiss him. Amasa was not on his guard against the dagger in Joab's hand, and Joab plunged it into his belly" (2 Sam. 20:9–10).

We do not know Joab's motivation. Perhaps he believed that Amasa had betrayed David. Or perhaps he just wanted revenge against the man who had displaced him. In any case, it was a classic case of a living contradiction.

A New Testament example is the behavior of Ananias and Sapphira (Acts 5:1–10). They appeared to give their all to Christ and the church but contradicted that appearance in their behavior. They pretended to give all the proceeds of the sale of a piece of their property but secretly withheld some. As Peter pointed out, what was the point of that? They were under no obligation to give all or any of their money. No doubt they sought the church's admiration by appearing to give it all. The contradiction was exposed, however, and they both died in disgrace.

In Joab's case, the contradiction was destructive to someone else; in Ananias and Sapphira's case, the contradiction was self-destructive. In Ray's case, the contradiction is both—in fact, it's destructive in three ways. It's destructive to Ray because we all need to be able to express our feelings to someone else; Ray is carrying the burden of having to deny something that is happening to him. It's also destructive to Jean; she feels shut out from a vital part of Ray's life. And it's destructive to their relationship, so destructive that Jean fears for their marriage. "At times," she says, "I feel as if Ray has gone into another room and locked the door. He excludes me and refuses to let me in."

Is Ray being honest with Jean? Keep in mind that he has not engaged in any overt lie. He has no intention and no desire to deceive Jean. Yet an honest marriage is more than the absence of blatant deceit. In an honest marriage, you don't throw your partner into perplexity and despair by living as a contradiction, even if your intentions are good.

VARIATIONS ON THE THEME

Ray is one kind of living contradiction, but he is not the only kind. For each variation we discuss, we want to underscore the point that we do not assume that the person who is a living contradiction *intends* to deceive. In the next section, we'll deal with the question of why a Christian would be a living contradiction; here, we want to show the various ways in which a spouse can be such a contradiction.

The Spouse with "Feelings in the Safe"

In our experience, Ray represents one of the more common kinds of living contradictions—a spouse with words and feelings that contradict each other. We call this the spouse with "feelings in the safe" because the person keeps his or her feelings hidden away from anyone else, and only he or she has the key to the contents of the safe. The feelings kept hidden are considered negative in some sense (no one we know tries to hide positive feelings like love and joy). The partner who tries to keep feelings hidden may do so by denying the negative feelings, affirming positive feelings that do not exist, or both. Jean gets both kinds of responses from Ray. "Sometimes I look at Ray, and I know that he's not feeling well or at least that he's bothered by something. He looks as if he's down in the mouth. So I ask him, 'How are you feeling today?' And he tells me that he's feeling fine. If I push him, and say, 'Are you sure?' he assures me that he's really okay. So sometimes I try a more direct approach. I say, 'You look glum today. Are you feeling down?' Then he'll tell me he doesn't feel down, that everything is okay."

As Jean's account illustrates, no matter how much we try verbally to present ourselves in a particular way, we can't really keep our feelings totally hidden—especially from our spouses, who may know us in some ways better than we know ourselves.

So the "feelings safe" isn't really safe in the sense of keeping the contents out of sight. We may deny that we are angry, but the crisp edge on our words will betray us. We may insist that we aren't discouraged, but the dullness in our eyes will contradict us. We may say that we are not hurt by our spouse, but the deepened lines of our face will say otherwise. We may disavow feelings of jealousy, but the fury within us will break out in our demeanor and crush our words.

We can control what we say, but we can never totally control our nonverbal signals. Perhaps God has made us that way in an effort to minimize the possibilities of secrets in marriage. Willing us to become one flesh, he made sure that we would always give off signals that would reveal something of our feelings even when our words give a different message.

In other words, the spouse who has trouble expressing his or her true feelings and who tries to deny those true feelings can't really pull it off. Indeed, it is for that very reason that the denial is destructive to the relationship— your spouse knows that something is wrong but doesn't know what it is. Jean spoke about her weariness with Ray's denial. "The problem is that I don't always know exactly what he's feeling, but I do know he's feeling something different from what he's telling me. When he's upset with me, for instance, he gets tight around his mouth. So I know he's upset. But if I say, 'Are you mad at me?' he'll just look puzzled—as if to say, Why in the world would you ask such a question?—and say no. So I know he's upset, but I don't know whether he's angry or hurt or disappointed or what. And I get tired of trying to drag it out of him."

Many people have trouble sharing their feelings with their spouses. In premarital counseling, one of the issues we explore is the extent to which each partner feels free to express feelings to the other. If one of them has difficulty, it's frequently the man, but some women also admit to the problem.

If you or your spouse has such difficulty, keep in mind that an honest sharing of feelings is crucial to building intimacy. Then work together on learning how to share your feelings. Here are two techniques we recommend.

First, reward your spouse whenever he or she shares feelings with you. If, for example, your spouse says, "I feel a little down today," don't respond with, "Oh, you shouldn't feel that way," or "But you have so much to be thankful for." At that point, your spouse doesn't need either a rebuke or a sermon on being grateful; he or she needs an appreciative and supportive ear. So you might say something like, "I noticed you looked down. I'm glad you told me; I need to know so I don't assume you're mad at me or disappointed with me about something. Do you know what has made you feel that way? What can I do to help?"

Second, have some regular but private marriage-enrichment sessions in which you practice sharing feelings. Choose a time when you can talk uninterruptedly for about a half hour. Then take turns and share your feelings with each other. Allow the spouse who doesn't have trouble talking about feelings to go first, to encourage the other to share honestly.

What kind of feelings do you share in these sessions? You have a number of possibilities.

- Choose some event or incident of the past and try to reconstruct how you felt at that time.
- Think about a particular kind of feeling—anger, joy, glumness, satisfaction, jealousy, pride, embarrassment, or disappointment—and talk about a time when you felt it keenly.
- Talk about how you are feeling at the moment or how you felt last night or try to give the full range of feelings you have experienced thus far in the day.
- Talk about positive feelings so that the sessions focus on more than the uncomfortable feelings many of us have trouble expressing.

Working together in this way, you can help the spouse who finds it difficult to express feelings to become more open and at the same time you will deepen your intimacy. Keep in mind that most people who find it difficult to talk about their feelings have been that way throughout their lives. Changing the pattern will take time. It may always be a bit of a battle to open the safe and let the feelings out. However, the rewards for doing so are well worth the battle.

The Spouse with a Blind Spot

A second variation of the living contradiction involves a contradiction between words and behavior. We call this the spouse with a blind spot because, once again, we make no assumption that the contradiction is intended or even recognized.

Amy works as a part-time waitress. She has a seven-year-old daughter and a husband, Frank, who is the foreman of a construction company. When Amy first spoke to us, she was both dismayed and perplexed: "I don't know what to do. Frank is a good man. You know we both are regular at church, and our faith is very important to us. But for the last few years, I feel disconnected from Frank. He just isn't a husband to me anymore. Don't misunderstand. He doesn't do anything bad, like abuse me. And he takes care of all our needs for food and that kind of thing. Yet he never touches me—I mean in a loving way. He never hugs me or even kisses me; we haven't made love in nearly a year. But he insists that nothing is wrong with him and that he loves me as much as ever."

How did Frank respond? He was unsettled by Amy's frankness, but basically he told us the same thing he had been saying to Amy when she complained to him. "I'm a good provider. Amy has a good home, and we have a good family. I love her and take care of her. She knows that. She thinks I'm involved with another woman, but I'm not that kind of guy. I know what's right. She doesn't understand how tired I am after work. I've got a lot of responsibility, and it's really stressful. When I get home, I need to rest and relax. Why can't she understand that?"

Verbally, Frank asserted his continuing love for Amy. But he had to admit that his behavior had changed toward her. He insisted, however, that he saw no contradiction between his behavior and his avowed love for Amy.

We agreed that work can sometimes sap a person's energy and diminish the sex drive—but for a whole year? Certainly he wouldn't be so weary that he couldn't hug or kiss Amy. As it turned out, Frank suffered from inhibited sexual desire, a problem that afflicts as many as half of all spouses at some time in their lives. One of the causes can be the fatigue that results from a stressful and demanding job.

Because he was embarrassed about, and did not understand, the problem, Frank said nothing to Amy or anyone else. Since he feared that if he hugged and kissed Amy, she would expect him to make love, he refrained from even those expressions of affection.

Frank was honest and correct in claiming that he still loved Amy as much as ever. However, because he couldn't bring himself to talk with her about his inhibited sexual desire, his behavior contradicted his words. Frank's secret rapidly eroded their intimacy. Fortunately, Amy sought help in time to stem the deterioration. Eventually, as a result of counseling, open discussion, and hard work, Frank's desire returned.

In the process of experiencing and working through his problem, Frank discovered the importance of an honest relationship. He came to realize two things. First, he learned that a dishonest relationship erodes and may even destroy intimacy. Second, he learned that an honest relationship enables husbands and wives to fulfill one of their important tasks—to help each other deal with problems.

Amy's help was not just nice to have. Frank *needed* Amy's help to overcome his problem. He needed her patience and understanding. He needed her encouragement. He needed her declarations of love in spite of his neglect. He needed her affirmations of respect and admiration in the face of what he considered an extremely humiliating affliction. Amy's acceptance of Frank's inhibited desire as a relatively common experience helped him to accept it too. Her ability to get beyond feeling that his behavior was a rejection of her enabled her to agree with Frank's insistence that his love for her had not waned. But none of this was possible while Frank kept his secret. Spouses can only help each other if they are willing to be honest.

Frank and Amy's story illustrates our point that a contradiction between words and behavior is not necessarily a case of intentional dishonesty. Few if any Christians would, like Joab, put on a facade of affection in order to be destructive. Nevertheless, the contradiction is still destructive. Whether or not the contradiction is intentional, it's important to recognize and deal with it.

Consider the destructiveness of the following situations:

- What she says: "I'm working long hours only to provide the best for my family."
- What her behavior says to her family: My job is more important to me than anything else. You should understand that and support me instead of complaining.
- What he says: "I accept my responsibility to be the head of my home. I will take proper care of my family."
- What his behavior says to his wife: You are incompetent and in need of my constant help. You could never make it without me.
- What she says: "I help my husband with all those social graces."
- What her behavior says to her husband: You never do anything right. Why are you such a clod?

These examples are just a few of the ways that words and behavior (which includes nonverbal signals) can contradict each other. You may neither intend nor desire to say to your spouse what your behavior is saying. Similarly, your spouse may neither intend nor desire to say to you what his or her behavior is saying. Unfortunately, neither of you will know what is meant unless you are willing to be honest with each other.

So what can you do if your spouse is a living contradiction? The problem requires a confrontation. Yet note the way in which Amy confronted Frank. When she began to discuss the problem, she first pointed out Frank's good points. She did not begin with an assault on either his motives or his behavior.

If you need to confront your spouse about a contradiction, begin by affirming your love and respect. Then point out that what you are saying is your *perception* of the situation (leaving the door open that you might be wrong or have only a partial understanding). Tell your spouse how you feel about what you see as a contradiction. Certainly, always ask your spouse what the two of you can do to deal with the issue.

Finally, keep in mind that blind spots are like keeping feelings in a safe—they tend to become habitual and will not quickly yield to change. Be patient and work with your spouse (and with a counselor if necessary). Maintain your confidence in the Lord, who promised that he has come, among other things, to proclaim "recovery of sight for the blind" (Luke 4:18). We don't think it's stretching his meaning to include in his promise those who suffer the kind of blind spots we have discussed in this section.

The Spouse with Two Faces

Two-faced? That sounds like blatant duplicity. Not necessarily. We use the term to refer to the spouse who has a public face and a private face that contradict each other. And, again, we assume that the contradiction is not a deliberate deception.

In its milder form, this contradiction takes the form of acts of graciousness for others that a person does not offer to his or her spouse. For example, a man may be considerate and sensitive about a female co-worker and at the same time be insensitive about his own wife. He may compliment a woman with whom he works about her work or her appearance while his wife starves for any kind of compliment about any aspect of her life.

Similarly, a woman may be very concerned about the problems and worries of other people. She may listen to others and express her understanding and support. Yet she may shrug off her husband's worries by telling him curtly that his worries are groundless and pointless.

In a more severe form, this contradiction is seen in the man who is congenial with outsiders but verbally or even physically abusive with his wife. We once lived near a minister of a small church. In his public life, the minister seemed to function well with his congregations. In his private life, he had another face, for his immediate neighbors could hear him periodically screaming at his family. The verbal abuse of his private face contradicted the patience and understanding of his public face.

We need to be cautious when thinking about this particular contradiction. To some extent, we're all somewhat different people in our private and public worlds. In our public lives we observe certain social conventions that aren't necessary in the home. We may avoid certain behavior at work because we want to protect our position.

For example, in one of our marriage-enrichment classes, a wife complained about her husband's congeniality at work and the irritation he expressed at home. His irritation was with a boss who was autocratic. When the boss made up his mind, he would tolerate no alternative suggestions or anything less than full support of his decision from his subordinates. So the husband kept quiet at work, but his frustration spilled out when he got home.

His wife understood the frustration and irritation that this work situation generated, but she questioned whether it was fair for him to vent his frustrations at home in such a harsh way.

Under the circumstances, we suggested that she try to put his behavior in a somewhat different perspective. "Actually, what your husband is doing is a compliment to you. He feels that he can express to you things that he can't express on his job. With you, he's safe. We all need to have someone with whom we can share our vexations in life. In a good marriage, that person is likely to be your spouse. It's just one more of the helpful things that spouses can do for each other."

Thus, in some cases the contradiction between the public and private face is appropriate or necessary. In other cases, it is neither. What, then, can you do if your spouse has two faces that are destructive to your marriage? Again, it will be necessary to confront him or her with the problem. And again, we suggest that you do so in the manner we outlined above. If the problem is very severe, as in the case of verbal or physical abuse, your spouse must have therapy. In our experience and research, we have found no cases of abusive spouses who changed merely by discussing the problem with their partner. Abusive people are notoriously quick to apologize and to promise an end to the abuse; but they are also quick to fall back into the same pattern.

CONTRADICTIONS AS A DEFENSE

Why do Christians get caught up in living contradictions? Many people who live contradictions are trying to defend something that's very important to them, namely, an image of themselves as "good Christian people." Forgetting that we are all sinners saved by grace, they define the good Christian person as one who does not experience negative emotions like anger, resentment, and depression or who does not exhibit negative behavior like insensitivity, selfishness, and abuse.

Let's return to Ray, for example. Ray is an active member of his church. He contributes in a variety of ways, from ushering to teaching classes. He is beginning to see the root of his problem in two factors. One is the fact that the difficulty he has in sharing his feelings is a lifelong problem; his childhood family never encouraged (and in some ways discouraged) him to express his feelings. Keeping his feelings to himself is a deeply ingrained habit.

The second factor, however, is his unrealistic image of what it means to be a good Christian: "In my mind, I know that Christians are not perfect people. But I just find it hard to admit that I could be angry with my wife. I don't want to be that way. And I find it hard to admit if I'm feeling depressed. Then I think to myself: 'I'm supposed to have the joy of God's salvation. Why should I feel this way? What's wrong with me?' I guess I try to stop thinking about the way I feel in the hope that it will go away. And it does eventually. But in the meantime, Jean wants to know what's going on, and I don't really want to tell her because it embarrasses me."

We don't like anyone, not even our spouses, to see us with all our weaknesses showing. Ford Maddox Ford, a turn-of-the-century novelist, once observed a constant factor in every marriage: "A desire to deceive the person with whom one lives as to some weak spot in one's character or in one's career. For it is intolerable to live constantly with one human being who perceives one's small meannesses. It is really death to do so—that is why so many marriages turn out unhappily."

We agree with Ford that few if any of us want to reveal our full range of weaknesses to our spouses. However, Ford was wrong when he said that revealing the weaknesses makes the marriage turn out unhappily. Quite the contrary is true, as Ray and Jean's story illustrates. Defending an ideal self-image can be an effective way to erode marital intimacy.

In some cases, the desire to defend our self-image can take a nasty turn and lead us to blame the other person for the weaknesses. For instance, those who verbally or physically abuse others typically blame the victims. The message is: "I'm basically a good person. The only reason I abuse you is because of the way you behave. You force me to abuse you."

To help us avoid becoming a living contradiction, we need to remember that God has called us not to defend our image but to protect and develop our marriages. The more consistent our words and feelings and behavior, the more easily we can nurture our marital relationships.

CHAPTER 4

Your Personal Package of Secrets

*I*n case you thought you could skip this chapter, you need to know that we each have our own package of secrets in marriage. We brought some of them with us when we entered marriage. Most of us are unaware of these secrets until something forces us to acknowledge them.

The kinds of things we will discuss in this chapter are not secrets in the sense that either spouse is deliberately hiding something but in the sense that the couple has never openly recognized and acknowledged the "secrets." However, the secrets affect the way spouses act and react to each other. They can result in conflict, often serious conflict, between a husband and wife. For that reason it's important to understand your personal package of secrets.

YOUR SECRET MARITAL AGREEMENT

Everyone who gets married has a secret prenuptial agreement. The agreement is composed of all those nonverbalized expectations you have with your partner. Some of those expectations may be perfectly appropriate. However, because you and your spouse have not openly recognized and acknowledged them, you could be headed for problems.

After you're married, that agreement may gradually change, only to be replaced by something new. Nevertheless, you will retain a secret marital agreement.

Kevin and Elsbeth discovered the perilous nature of their secret agreements after five years of marriage. They are both college graduates, and they both work in business. They share the various household responsibilities. They also love to travel and try to plan for some new place to visit each year.

In their fifth year, their marriage suddenly ran into trouble. Kevin was ready to buy a home and begin their family. Elsbeth was reluctant. She found the prospect of traveling more appealing than a mortgage, and she wasn't sure she was sufficiently established in her career to begin having children.

For the first time in their marriage, Kevin and Elsbeth began to argue strongly over money. He wanted to save for a down payment on a home. He accused Elsbeth of "going crazy" with credit cards. Worse, he accused her of reneging on the understanding they had before they got married: to begin their family within the first five years of marriage.

Elsbeth vigorously denied that she had violated any such agreement. She insisted that she wanted a home and children as much as Kevin did. "We agreed only that we would have them," she told him, "not that we would have them in five years."

Kevin reminded Elsbeth that he was already thirty-five years old. "If I wait another five years, I'll be retired before my children are grown."

Elsbeth and Kevin are the victims of their secret prenuptial agreements. His agreement was that they would have children by the time he was thirty-five. Her agreement was that they would have children after they had traveled extensively and she was at the point in her career where she could take time off. Unfortunately neither had actually told the other about these "agreements."

Elsbeth and Kevin's marriage will probably survive. Yet they could have avoided the stress they are experiencing if they had made their expectations clear to each other from the start. Instead, like all of us, each of them simply assumed that the other had the same expectations.

The secret agreements of another couple, Ted and Bonnie, did not surface until twenty years after their marriage. Through two decades of marriage, Ted and Bonnie seemed to be the ideal couple. Ted prospered professionally, while Bonnie cared for their home and three children. However, after their third child started high school, Bonnie became restless and got a job as an elementary-school teacher. That's when the difficulties began.

According to Ted, Bonnie changed completely, and he didn't like the changes. "Bonnie no longer takes care of the house the way she used to," Ted complained. "She hardly ever cooks my favorite meals any more. I feel as if she prefers her job to me. This is not what I bargained for at all when we married. It may be selfish, but I wanted—and still want—a wife who takes care of me as my mother took care of my dad. My work demands nearly all of my energy, and when I get home, I just have nothing left to give."

Bonnie, on the other hand, had a very different secret agreement when she married: "We married just after college, and I immediately got pregnant. I was more than willing to stay home and raise a family as well as support Ted in his work. And I did a good job of it. Ted's business is a success, and the children are happy, well adjusted, and intelligent. In the back of my mind, however, I always knew that my time would come and that I would eventually pursue my own professional career. That's what I've done. At this point, I find that teaching is much more fulfilling than cleaning the bathroom grout or cooking a gourmet meal. I know that Ted isn't thrilled by the new me, but I really think that he would like the change if he'd let himself. But his only concern is about what I'm not doing for him. What I'd like from him is support and a little help around the house. After all, it's his house too, isn't it? I feel as if I've done all the work in this marriage and carried more than my share of the load. And that's unfair; now it's his turn to carry an equal load."

Ted and Bonnie's secret agreement didn't emerge until rather late in their marriage. Essentially the conflict over what constituted a fair division of labor in their family forced their differing expectations into the open. In a counseling session, both agreed they felt that marriage should be a "fifty-fifty" proposition. Ted maintained that he was responsible for the financial well-being of the family and that Bonnie's responsibility was to take care of their home and family. Bonnie, on the other hand, argued that, at this stage of their lives, it was time to share the financial and family tasks.

For the health of Ted and Bonnie's relationship, it was critical, first of all, that they confront their secret agendas of the past, explore how these were affecting their present relationship, and find ways to accommodate their differing expectations. It was also necessary for them to deal with the issue of equity in their relationship. A common myth many couples believe is that marriage is a fifty-fifty arrangement. Such strict equality, in our judgment, is both unnecessary and unrealistic. The couples in our study of long-term marriages said that spouses should each be willing to give *more* than fifty-fifty. In the long run, they may well achieve a sense of equality. What's more important, however, is that each partner senses fairness rather than strict equality in the division of labor.

For some people, of course, fairness means, "I expect to give no more than you do to this relationship. I'm keeping count to make sure that happens." For the Christian, however, fairness means, "I'm not keeping count. I trust you to do your share, just as you trust me to do mine. Sometimes I'll do more because you need extra help, and sometimes you'll do more because I need extra help." It wasn't until Ted and Bonnie adopted this principle in their relationship that their marriage again regained the vitality of its early years.

In essence, then, the experiences of Ted and Bonnie as

well as Elsbeth and Kevin show that through our secret marital agreements:

- Each of us brings expectations to the marriage and develops new expectations as the years pass.
- Each of us assumes that our spouse shares those expectations.
- Each of us acts and reacts as if our spouse knows and agrees with the expectations we have.

To be sure, we will share many of our spouse's expectations. Those we don't share are the ones that comprise each spouse's personal package of secrets. And it is those personal packages that can threaten the marriage.

Expectations that Threaten

Some expectations are normal and undoubtedly shared. When you got married, you probably expected your spouse to be faithful, to continue to love you, to be honest with you, and to do his or her share in building a good marriage and home. Such expectations are universal; people everywhere have them.

Other expectations are a part of the culture. In biblical times, for example, any woman would expect to become a mother. The Hebrews and other Semitic people did not consider a woman to be fully human until she bore a son. No Hebrew woman would think of doing what some modern women do: declare that she preferred to remain childless. On the contrary, some of the more moving stories of the Bible deal with childless women like Sarah (Abraham's wife) and Hannah (Samuel's mother), who praise God mightily when they are finally blessed with the gift of a child.

One of the difficulties facing married couples today is that our culture has few distinct cultural expectations. As little as a generation ago, those who married were likely to have shared or at least have had similar expectations about such things as marital roles, whether to have children, and the division of household responsibilities. Now young people come with more personal than universal or cultural expectations. Unfortunately, they may also assume that their spouses come with the same personal expectations that they themselves have.

Why Expectations Threaten

Expectations are not threatening simply because they are personal or even because they are different from the spouse's. They are threatening to marriage when they are a part of your personal package of secrets and you continue to act and react to your spouse as if you both agreed on the expectations.

For example, Rick and Diana came to counseling after three years of marriage. Both of them looked hurt and perplexed. Diana volunteered to talk about their problem first. "Rick and I have gotten to the point where we can't even seem to talk about what's bothering us. We just don't connect. I don't think either of us really knows what's going on with the other. Like the other night. On Friday nights, we always try to do something special. Rick brought home some pizza, and I had baked his favorite cake. I was really eager to see him, and he came in all irritated with me. He says he tore his shirt getting out of the car because I had parked my car too close to the center of the garage, and he couldn't get his door open far enough."

Rick's irritation made Diana furious. But it was more than the one incident: "He always blames me when anything goes wrong in his life. It was *my* fault that he tore his shirt. Like it was *my* fault when we had a flat tire and didn't get to his parents' house on time for dinner. And *my* fault when he cracked a tooth . . ."

Diana began to cry softly. Rick shifted in his chair and gave his perspective on the problem: "I just don't see it as a big deal. Okay, so I get a little irritated when things don't go the way I'd like. I blow up. But then I settle down and everything's fine. Why make a big deal out of it? We keep arguing over things that aren't really that important. Diana's just too sensitive. She knew I had a problem with my temper when we got married. I don't know why it bothers her so much now. Besides, we agreed a year ago that I would work on controlling it and she would help me. And I'm actually controlling it better than I used to. So why all of a sudden is it such a problem?"

Diana agreed that Rick was in better control of his temper than when they had first met. She admitted that he had improved considerably since they had agreed to work together on helping him control it. However, it was that very agreement that led to their problem now. As it turned out, each of them was violating the other's secret agreement.

In discussing what to do about his temper, Diana and Rick had simply agreed that he would work on it and she would be patient and help him in any way she could. This was their overt agreement. But each had a secret agreement as well—not secret in the sense of withholding it from the other, but simply in the sense of not making it explicit.

Diana's secret agreement went like this: "I will be patient and help you work on your problem with your temper if you will agree not to allow it to become an attack on me." One of the reasons Diana was anxious for Rick to control his temper was that she was tired of feeling victimized by it. She assumed that their agreement meant that even though he might still have angry outbursts, he would at least not blame her when things went wrong. Diana was acting in ways consistent with that agreement and was getting very upset when Rick violated it.

Rick's secret agreement, on the other hand, went like this: "I will work on controlling my temper if you remain patient and continue to love me even when I say things that upset you." Rick knew that he hurt Diana when he got angry and that he said things that he didn't really mean. He assumed that she understood this and would overlook it as long as his outbursts were becoming less frequent. He assumed that Diana agreed with him and was perplexed because Diana kept violating the agreement.

Once Rick and Diana understood the problem of their secret agreements, they were able to work through the difficulties. After a few months of effort, their marriage was on much firmer ground. Rick had gained a new appreciation for the way in which the tongue can be "a fire, a world of evil among the parts of the body" (James 3:6). He was learning to direct his anger at things instead of people.

"Would you believe it?" he said one day. "We had another flat on the way to my parents' house!" However, this time he blamed the street instead of Diana.

Diana, at the same time, gained a new appreciation for the many ways in which she could fulfill her calling to love her husband (Titus 2:4). When Rick did lose his temper, she reassured him of her unbroken love and support. When he was in an anger-provoking situation but kept his temper, she praised him.

As long as their personal marital agreements remained secret, Rick and Diana each felt betrayed and perplexed. Once the secret agreements were out in the open, they could not only accept them but also use them to enrich their marriage.

THE HIDDEN-NEEDS SYNDROME

Bill and Vicki had experienced one of the most devastating things that can happen to any parent—their three-year-old daughter died of a rare disease that struck suddenly and led to her death in a matter of weeks. We were with these two people throughout the illness and death and in the months following as they tried to come to terms with their grief.

The divorce rate among couples who have a child die is high. It seems that the spouse's presence is a continual, painful reminder of the loss. Some people try to cope with it by escaping that continual reminder. So we were not surprised when Bill and Vicki came to us about their marital problems. As Christians, they didn't want to compound the loss of their daughter with the breakup of their marriage. Yet they felt increasingly alienated from each other and needed help if they were to stay together.

At one session, Vicki said, "At times I feel so empty. I just want Bill to take me in his arms and hold me tight. I want him to hold me for a long time so I know he's there for me."

"Have you told him that?" we asked. There was a brief silence. Then Vicki said, "No. I want him to know when I need him." And we immediately realized that, besides their other problems, their marriage was under attack from the hidden-needs syndrome.

The Silent Killer

High blood pressure is the silent killer of bodies; it's "silent" because it offers no clear evidence to the victim of its presence. The hidden-needs syndrome is a silent killer of marriages; it's "silent" because one or both of the victims are unaware of it.

In essence, the person with the hidden-needs syndrome holds the following set of attitudes:

1. I have needs that you can fulfill.
2. You should know those needs.
3. If you truly love me, you will respond to my needs.
4. I need not bother to test these assumptions.

True, Vicki was hurting. But so was Bill. In any case, to assume that someone else should know all of your needs and respond to them is to expect that person to be like God. Bill was perfectly willing, even eager, to hold Vicki when she needed him. It was humanly impossible, however, for him to know exactly when she had the need.

For Bill and Vicki, the problem of hidden needs appeared in a time of severe trauma. But it isn't only the marriage that has been struck by a crisis that is vulnerable to hidden needs. These silent killers attack couples in many different ways. The hidden-needs syndrome is present in the following kinds of situations:

She: Dinner is ruined. Why didn't you call me if you knew you were going to be late?

He: But I didn't know. I got caught in heavy traffic.

She: Couldn't you have stopped somewhere and phoned?

He: I kept thinking it would break up.

She: I made a special meal for you tonight. I really worked hard on it. I needed you to be on time.

He: Why didn't you tell me? Maybe I could have left early.

She: You seem really irritable tonight. What's wrong?

He: (sharply) Nothing.

She: Something's wrong. Why don't you talk about it?

He: I'm just tired. As soon as I get home from work, you bombard me with all that stuff about living closer to your parents and buying a different house. Why can't you leave it alone for a while?

She: But we agreed that we have to make the decisions soon. I don't understand why that should upset you. I just want to talk about what we're going to do.

He: But I'm tired. I've had tough decisions to make all day. I sure don't want to come home and make more of them. I need a break from having to think about decisions.

She: Why didn't you say so? I don't mind talking about them some other time.

Most of us like the notion of a spouse who knows and responds to our unspoken needs. But that's beyond the capacity of any spouse. "Ask," taught Jesus, "and it will be given to you" (Matt. 7:7). "You do not have," wrote James, "because you do not ask God" (James 4:2). If the God who knows all of our needs still requires us to ask, how can we expect our spouses to respond to hidden needs?

The Courage to Ask

The real problem with the hidden-needs syndrome, then, is not the inability of your spouse to know and respond to your needs; rather it's your hesitation or reluctance to tell him or her what your needs are. Why do we hesitate simply to tell each other what we need? Why, for instance, was Vicki reluctant? As it turned out, in those painful days of grief, she needed to know that their loss would not drive him away from her. In her mind, if he knew what she needed and responded to it, those gestures would assure her of his continuing love and commitment.

In many cases, the unwillingness to tell one's spouse what one needs is rooted in this misguided desire to test the spouse's love. In other cases, the reluctance may stem from embarrassment. The man who didn't want to make decisions when he came in from work may have an unrealistic image of himself; he might think that greeting his wife with his desire for rest and chitchat rather than any serious talk would be a confession of weakness. After all, as a man, he should be able to handle anything.

Or the reluctance to share needs with our spouse may be rooted in the fear of rejection. Some of this was true in Vicki's case. Knowing that Bill was hurting, too, she feared that he might not have wanted to hold her when she asked. His rejection at this time would have been unbearable to her.

Mindy, another young wife who feared rejection, talked about the problem in terms of her need for affection: "We have a good marriage on the whole. But I wish we had more affection. I mean the holding hands, hugging kind of affection. The trouble is, if I touch my husband, he will want to make love. And sometimes I just want the touching. You know, holding each other and feeling close, but not always having to make love as a result."

Mindy should talk to her husband about her needs. Yet she's afraid that he will get angry and interpret what she says to mean that she doesn't want to make love with him as often as they do. Rather than risk what she sees as a possible rejection, she says nothing and lets her needs go unfulfilled.

Unfortunately, that is precisely the alternative you face if you let the hidden-needs syndrome go unchecked. That is, you either break the syndrome by talking with your spouse openly about your needs, or you let the needs go unfulfilled and risk the deterioration of your marriage.

ATTACKING THE SECRETS

We want to stress that we all have expectations and we all have needs. However, when those expectations and needs are a part of your personal package of secrets, they can trouble your marriage. And as the couples we have written about in this chapter well illustrate, it wasn't until conflict occurred that they fully realized their own or each other's expectations.

Fortunately, you have alternatives. That is, you don't have to wait until a secret marital agreement or a hidden need causes a problem before you deal with it. The following exercises can help to open up your packages and thereby minimize conflict arising from secrets in your marriage.

Exercise One

First, select some aspect of your relationship in which you have some tension or conflict or in which you feel that you and your spouse are not connecting in the way you would like. Then each of you make a list, writing down as completely as possible what you would say about that aspect if you were to draw up a contract of expectations. That is, exactly what do you expect out of yourself and your spouse? Once you each have written up your contracts, share and discuss them. Then try to write out a final form of the agreement that is acceptable to both of you.

Suppose, for instance, that you and your spouse have some tensions over the budget: One of you wants to save more than the other. Let's say that the husband is a free spender and the wife likes to keep the budget under tight control. Each writes out a personal statement of expectations. The statements might look like this:

Husband: I expect to be able to spend money periodically on things that I would like for us to have and on places that I would like us to go. I expect to do that without your making me feel guilty or irresponsible. I will try to keep my spending within reasonable limits, and I will try to help you save a certain amount each month.

Wife: I expect to save some money each month for our future needs and emergencies. I expect to do that without feeling that I am just a penny pincher. I expect you to appreciate that I'm concerned about our financial well-being. I will try to be understanding of your needs and balance our saving with a certain amount of spending on things that please you.

As each spouse looks at what the other has written, you may be surprised to some extent. "I didn't realize that I made you feel guilty about your spending," the wife may say.

"I didn't know that you felt unappreciated; I didn't mean to imply that you were just being tight and stingy," the husband may say. They are now able to work out a resolution, a final draft of their new agreement. Their personal packages of secrets will be a little emptier.

Exercise Two

This exercise is based on a suggestion we make to couples in premarital counseling: Learn to engage in your own regular marriage enrichment. You can use some of the kinds of experiences you would have at a formal marriage-enrichment weekend to program an ongoing enrichment for yourselves. The following exercise is one example.

Set aside some private time each week when you can talk with each other without interruption. Even fifteen minutes would be enough for a useful exercise, though a half hour or more would be better. We suggest that you sit facing each other and look at each other as you talk. Walking together and talking, or sitting on a couch and talking are also possible, but they don't have the connecting power of looking into each other's eyes as you talk.

If you have been having some tension or disagreements about a particular topic, explore that topic in the terms we have discussed in this chapter. Allow a third of the time you have for one spouse to talk about the issue without interruption or comment from the other, a third of the time for the other spouse to do the same, and a third for discussion.

Let's say, for example, that you have been disagreeing about the amount of time you are spending with your parents. Your spouse thinks you are still tied to your parents' apron strings, but you feel an obligation to honor your aging parents by spending whatever time you can with them. It may be a secret agreement or a hidden need is compounding the issue. Each of you should talk about it in something like the following terms:

- "My parents expect me . . ."
- "When I spend time with my parents, I expect you to . . ."
- "When I think of my parents, I realize that I need . . ."
- "With regard to your parents, I expect you to . . ."
- "The reason I object to the time you spend with your parents is that I need . . ."

In other words, try to identify not only the expectations you have for your spouse and yourself but also the needs you both have; you may not have articulated these needs to your spouse, or you may not have fully thought them out for yourself. Since it's sometimes difficult for us to pull these secrets out of our packages, the discussion should include time for each of you to respond to the other. For instance, you might say to your spouse: "You said that as far as my spending time with my parents you expect . . . But I feel that you also expect . . . Do you think that's a fair assessment?" And your spouse might say: "You say your parents expect . . . Is that really their expectation, or is it more your need?"

The point of the exercise is *not* to challenge each other but to work together to uncover the secrets. You can help each other to identify expectations and needs that may be difficult for you to recognize. The approach is not, "I know what I expect and I know what I need and I'm willing to lay them out for you." Rather, the approach is, "I know something of what I expect and something of what I need, and I'd like to hear what you have to say about my expectations and needs so that we can both get a clearer understanding of them."

Exercise Three

If you are not having tension or arguments over a particular topic, you can follow the procedure used above and engage in some preventive enrichment. That is, let each spouse take turns in talking to the other without interruption, then discuss what each has said. A good place to begin is by exploring the issues that typically are either a source of strength or a challenge in most marriages. For example, the issue of communication is vital to building an intimate relationship. You need to talk often enough that you feel connected with each other. You need to talk about the things that concern, interest, and bother both of you. You need small talk as well as discussions about serious matters.

Some excellent questions to help you begin an exploration of your communication patterns as well as your needs and expectations about communication are:

- Am I satisfied with the amount and kind of communication that we have?
- Are we open with each other?
- Do we disclose meaningful things about ourselves— our thoughts, feelings, fears, and joys—to each other?
- Does my spouse fulfill my need to have someone who really listens to me?
- Do I feel that I am fulfilling my spouse's need to have someone who truly listens?

Note our concern, here, with listening as an aspect of communication. We once heard a salesperson say that the problem with most people who work in sales is that they have two mouths and one ear. Many people believe that their spouses also fit that description. Effective communication demands reciprocity; that is, each spouse must actively listen as well as verbally respond. Chapter 11 will give some detailed help about these crucial aspects of communication. What is important, at this point, is that you use these questions to stimulate your thinking as you try to identify your expectations, needs, and secret agreements.

CHAPTER 5

The Parental Spouse

In his epic poem *The Odyssey*, one of Homer's characters advises another never to tell a woman all he knows. A man may tell a woman some things, he notes, but "some he should cover up."

This advice illustrates well the *parental approach* to male-female relationships. Parents never tell their children everything. In an effort to protect their children, they select what things to tell them. They may, for example, give a more optimistic picture of life than one would get by reading the daily papers. They may paint a rosier picture of family finances than is justified by the realities of income and expenses. They may present a more idealistic portrait of their own relationship than is justified by the number of disagreements they have.

Because our parents, and other adults to whom our parents entrusted us, were selective, we all grew up protected from some of the harder aspects of life, believing that fairy tales represented something true about the adult world. When we marry, however, we must leave our parents and be united with each other (Gen. 2:24). The command indicates that the marital relationship is different from the parental one. Tragically, some people confuse the two.

THE PARENTAL SPOUSE: A TRAGEDY IN TWO ACTS

We would like to tell you in some detail about one of the most unusual marriages we have encountered. We call it a tragedy in two acts because the marriage itself can be divided into two radically different time periods. For the first twenty years of their union, Warren and Iris had what seemed to be a solid Christian marriage. For the last three years, they have hung on to what seems to be an irreparably shattered relationship.

Warren is a businessman with high aspirations. Iris is a stay-at-home mom who has never worked outside the home. Early on, they had agreed that Iris would stay at home and raise their family. They have three children: the two youngest are in their teens, while the oldest is a college undergraduate.

Throughout the first twenty years of their marriage, Warren and Iris were very active in their church. For a number of years, he was a deacon, and she taught Sunday school. In their twenty-first year, Iris announced that she had a number of "family concerns" that would keep her from continuing her teaching. Iris's sudden decision surprised the church-school leaders. However, they also agreed that Iris deserved a sabbatical, expressed the hope that the family concerns were nothing serious, and assumed that once she had gotten her children through adolescence, she would return to teaching.

In their twenty-second year of marriage, Iris came to us for the first time. She was extremely tense. "I have to do something," she began. We assumed that she would talk about some kind of problem with the children. Instead, she said, "I don't think I can live with Warren anymore."

Her statement was startling because as far as anyone else could tell, she and Warren had a strong marriage. For twenty years, at least, they had given no one any hint of serious problems in their relationship. In fact, in our initial counseling sessions, Iris herself insisted that for the first twenty years no major problems had marred their marriage.

Usually, a severe disruption in a relationship has a history. In the case of Iris and Warren, the disruption seemingly occurred in a single day. Before that day, which she called "the day my blinders came off," Iris believed they had a satisfying marriage and family life. "We had always talked easily with each other about all sorts of things. We enjoyed doing the same kinds of things. Before the kids were born, we camped together and continued to do it after we had children. We both liked art and went together to museums and galleries. We had no serious quarrels over how to raise the children. I think they're quite happy and well adjusted. Now they are beginning to suspect that something is wrong, but they still don't know how serious it is."

With so much going for them, what happened? In essence, Warren has been a parental spouse throughout their marriage. But Iris did not know it until near their twentieth anniversary. On the day her "blinders came off," Iris discovered what he had been doing and felt overwhelmed with anger. "He betrayed me," she insists. "What he did is just as bad as if he had been unfaithful to me with another woman."

Worse, she feels that Warren continues to betray her even though he knows how much his behavior hurts her. This is Iris's story, beginning on the infamous day: "I was planning our vacation. I thought that since our twentieth anniversary was also coming up, we should celebrate it in some special way by taking a unique vacation. By now, our assets were such that we could afford something special. Since the kids were no longer going with us, it wouldn't even be that expensive.

"Warren always handled all our finances. But I wanted to surprise him. So I dug out the checkbook from his desk to make a down payment to the travel agent. When I looked at the balance, I saw we had only a couple hundred dollars in the checking account. I hated to draw money out of savings, but I desperately wanted to surprise Warren, so I looked around for the savings-account book. I couldn't find it. I then called the bank and asked if it would be possible to transfer some funds from our savings into the checking account. They told me that they were sorry but we didn't have a savings account with them, only a checking account.

"I felt a little uneasy but decided that Warren must have set up the savings at another bank. I went back to his desk and searched some more. I found no account book, but I did see a couple of notices of bills—large bills—past due.

"Now I really started to feel panic. What was going on? I thought about it a while, wondering what to do. I started to call Warren at work. However, I decided to wait until he got home. I looked at the past-due bills again. I hadn't even noticed where they were from, only the amount. It turned out that one was from a clinic that had done some tests on Warren. The panic returned. Warren was sick? He didn't even tell me? Was he dying or something?

"I couldn't stand it. I called him at work and said I had to know immediately what was happening. At first, he sounded a little hurt that I had gone through his desk. But he could tell how upset I was, so he told me the tests showed that he was okay. He hadn't told me about them beforehand because he didn't want to worry me. And he forgot about telling me afterward because he felt it wasn't necessary.

"I was so relieved about the tests that I didn't press him on the savings. When he got home that night, I told him that I wanted to know, that I had a right to know, if he was having a health problem. He promised never to keep it secret again. Then I asked about a special trip for our anniversary. He agreed. I told him I had one in mind and asked him to give me the money for the down payment.

"That's when I got my second shock. It turned out that we were broke. Broke! After twenty years of marriage. And I knew nothing about it. We have no savings. We live day to day with Warren playing musical chairs with the bills. He's squandered everything, including the inheritance I got from my parents. And this has been going on for years. I can't live with this man anymore."

When we talked with Warren, he basically agreed with Iris's account. He gave us a few more details. "Most of my work is speculative. I can make a lot of money quickly, and I can lose a lot quickly. The past ten years haven't been good ones for me. Iris doesn't even know yet the full extent of our situation. I haven't told her about the second mortgage I took out on the house or the money that I owe a former partner."

How could Warren keep the financial problems a secret from Iris for ten years? What is more important is *why*? He sees the issue as a very simple one: "I didn't want to upset her. She worries about that kind of thing, so I've never told her. I thought I could replace her inheritance money before she ever found out about it, but my business deals just haven't paid off.

"I've taken care of Iris all these years. She's never had to worry about anything. And it's not just the money or my health. I also took care of things with the kids and never told her."

Warren hopes that when Iris "cools down," she will realize how fortunate she has been to have a man who has been so protective. However, Iris hasn't cooled down for three years. She is more determined than ever to leave Warren. She isn't sure how to break the news to the children. Yet she is sure of one thing: She cannot live with a man who continues to treat her like a child.

ONE SET OF PARENTS IS AMPLE

Parents who love and nurture us are invaluable. But one set is ample. When a spouse also tries to act as a parent, the results are likely to range anywhere from disconcerting to disastrous. The reason is simple: A parental spouse deprives you of becoming the functioning adult that God intends for you to be. By the time you are married, you need to "put childish ways behind" you (1 Cor. 13:11). A parental spouse impedes rather than helps that process.

A parental spouse treats you like a dependent rather than a partner. When someone treats you like a child, especially someone who is very important in your life, you may become more childish in your behavior. Think, for example, about the marriage of King Ahab and Jezebel. At one point, Ahab coveted Naboth's vineyard, but Naboth refused to sell his land. Ahab, like a prototypical childish adult, went home and sulked in his bed, refusing to eat. Jezebel, like a parental spouse, said to him: "Is this how you act as king over Israel? Get up and eat! Cheer up. I'll get you the vineyard of Naboth the Jezreelite" (1 Kings 21:7). Jezebel wrote letters in Ahab's name, ordering some prominent citizens to secure witnesses who would say that Naboth had cursed both God and the king. Then, she told the citizens to take Naboth out and stone him to death. The citizens obeyed, and Ahab was able to get the vineyard he wanted.

Ahab and Jezebel were not partners in marriage. Rather, as the stronger of the two, Jezebel played the parental spouse. As the weaker of the two, Ahab played the dependent, childish spouse. And the outcome was disastrous, both for them and for people like Naboth, who were victimized by their unholy union.

Ahab's sulking in bed and the subsequent death of Naboth is an example of how severely destructive a parent-child marital relationship can be. At the very least, however, a parental spouse will retard the growth of his or her partner. This happens because the parental spouse deprives the other of the growth that comes from making important decisions.

One of the reasons that Iris is so angry with Warren is that he never gave her the option of participating in the decision-making process. "He says he wanted to protect me. But I never asked for, and certainly didn't want, that kind of protection. I want to decide for myself whether, and how much, to worry about his health. And I want to have a say in any decisions about how to handle our financial situation.

"He may think that he was protecting me, but he has lied to me. He's treated me like a child or one of his employees instead of his wife."

In some ways, Iris sounds like an adolescent rebelling against overprotective parents. Perhaps that's only to be expected, since Warren has in many respects treated her like a child for two decades. Eventually, the parental spouse is likely to face such a rebellion. Warren survived for so long only because he had managed to keep his parental ways a secret.

VARIATIONS ON THE THEME

There are two basic types of parental spouses: paternal and maternal. Warren is what we call a paternal spouse. The paternal spouse focuses on *protection*, which is the traditional responsibility of the male. The maternal spouse focuses on *nurturing*, which is the traditional emphasis of the female. This is not to say, however, that whenever we find a parental spouse, the male is paternal and the female is maternal. A husband can be either a paternal or maternal spouse, as can a wife. We need to look a bit more closely at each of these types to understand this point and to see in more detail the kind of behavior involved in each.

The Paternal Spouse

The paternal spouse seeks to protect his or her partner from such things as worry, difficult decisions, emotional upset, and troublesome situations. To achieve such a goal, of course, the paternal spouse necessarily keeps a certain number of matters secret, as Warren amply illustrated.

Sometimes we can detect the makings of a paternal spouse in premarital counseling. David, a successful real-estate broker, fell in love with Julie, who worked in the business office of a large department store. David and Julie were members of the same church and had lived in the same city all their lives. They were similar in virtually every way except one: he was forty and she was twenty-eight.

They didn't mind the twelve-year age difference. They were compatible and very much in love. In premarital counseling, their relationship seemed to be an exceptionally strong one—until we began to talk about roles. Julie believed in shared decision making; David believed a husband made decisions in important matters and a wife respected his decisions. When we asked David to give an example of what he had in mind, he replied, "Well Julie is a very caring person. And that's good. I know a Christian should be caring. But she's also naïve. She'll talk to strangers who come up to her on the street and try to help them."

"That's not the only thing that bothers you," Julie interjected. "You don't even want me to have male friends where I work."

David acknowledged that it troubled him for Julie to have such friendships. On further exploration, we realized that David was already playing the role of a paternal husband. He said that he based his feelings on the fact that he had more experience than Julie did. He knew, he insisted, what some of those "so-called male friends" really wanted from her. So he had decided to protect her from getting involved in a situation that could be troublesome.

We pointed out to David that Julie was, after all, twenty-eight years old. She was an adult, a very competent adult at that. After a number of additional counseling sessions, David began to work on his paternal approach to marriage. Julie is grateful. "I hadn't thought that much about it before we came to counseling because I was delirious with love. But I realize now that if we had gotten married without addressing that issue, we would be having serious problems now. I couldn't stand for David to treat me as if I were some kind of child."

As we pointed out before, it isn't only men who behave in a paternal fashion. Women can also try to be too protective of their husbands. We know a husband who feels very cheated since his wife of twenty-one years died after a long illness. While his wife was in the hospital during the final days of her life, she kept telling her husband that the results of tests showed she was finally getting better. It was a shock to him when she died. Their daughter knew the reason. "Mom always tried to protect Dad. I wasn't as fooled as he was by what she was saying. She didn't tell me she was dying, but she didn't tell me she was getting better either. But all the years they were married, she tried to protect him from anything that would upset him."

Of course, she didn't really protect him. He was quite angry for a long time after her death. He, like Iris, felt as if he had been treated like a child. "I had a right to know," he says. And he still regrets that he didn't have a chance to talk with her about some things that he would have talked about if he had known she was dying.

These illustrations make an important point: while it's natural to want to protect your spouse from hurtful things and undue stress, you can cross the line from being appropriately protective to being harmfully paternal. However, not all protectiveness is wrong. How, then, can you tell when you have crossed the line?

Certainly, keeping secrets is one indication that you have become paternal rather than appropriately protective. Thus, it is protective to discuss with your spouse the hazards of dealing with strangers or people of the opposite sex, then to trust your spouse to deal with the situation; it is paternal simply to insist that your spouse not deal with strangers or have friends of the opposite sex without trusting his or her ability to deal with the situation.

Another indication is based on the Golden Rule: "So in everything, do to others what you would have them do to you" (Matt. 7:12). That is, ask yourself: If the roles were reversed, would I want my spouse to do what I am doing in this situation? Would you feel that your spouse was being paternal if he or she did what you are doing? Don't answer the question too quickly. Our capacity for self-deception is boundless. Yet carefully and prayerfully applying the Golden Rule can help you avoid being paternal and free you to be appropriately protective.

The Maternal Spouse

The maternal spouse focuses on nurture, attempting to shape the partner's attitudes and behavior by directives, rewards, and continual expressions of concern. In other words, the maternal spouse, like the paternal, treats the spouse like a child in various ways—telling the partner what he or she should do and using various methods to insure that the spouse will comply.

To underscore the fact that either the husband or wife can be either kind of parental spouse, we will use the case of a male, maternal spouse here. Fred was married to Virginia for three years when his maternalism brought them to the counselor's office. Fred was wide-eyed and innocent: "I don't know why we're here. I think we have a good marriage. I've never done anything in my life to harm Virginia. Now, all of a sudden, she seems to think that I've been mistreating her."

Virginia looked at him with disbelief for a moment, then began her side of the story. "Fred can't seem to understand what I've been telling him for the past six months. Sure, we've had a good marriage. But that's because I've been a good little girl for three years. He's always telling me what to do. If I obey, I get my candy. If I don't, I get punished in some way until I do."

Virginia went on to describe the incident that made her realize how much she had endured from her maternal husband. Fred once told her that she needed to improve her housecleaning. Compared to his mother, she was "sloppy." Compared to her mother, she pointed out, she was "immaculate." When she balked at his suggestion, pointing out that their friends thought their house quite clean and comfortable, he got cold and distant. He said very little and constantly did things—like pick up a little piece of lint off the carpet—that reminded her of her "sloppiness."

Finally, one Saturday when Fred was out golfing, she spent the entire day cleaning the house. When he came home, she asked him if it now met his standards. He smiled, kissed her, and told her she was a good wife. He took her out for dinner and became warm and communicative again. Instead of feeling good, Virginia was furious. "I began to think of how this was so typical of our marriage. His punishment for my bad behavior and reward for my good behavior were so obvious that it opened my eyes. I don't have a husband, I thought to myself, I have a parent—one who is more manipulative than my own parents ever were. I might not have realized it if I hadn't stubbed my toe while I was vacuuming. I was hurt and suddenly very angry. I remember saying out loud, 'Here I am working, and he's out having fun on the golf course. What's going on?'"

The more she thought about it, the more Virginia was convinced that what was going on was inappropriate. She was right. Among other things, Fred was trying to shape her in terms of his secret premarital agreement: "I will love you and be faithful to you if you live up to the standards of my mother." Fred himself was aware that he constantly compared Virginia to his mother. Moreover, he regarded this as legitimate because he had idealized his mother. As a result, he expected Virginia to do everything the way his mother had done it. He expected her to greet him just as his mother greeted his father each day, to cook the kind of meals his mother cooked, to keep house the way his mother did, to relate to guests the way he had observed his mother doing, and so forth.

Fred had never specifically said to Virginia that his mother was his standard of comparison until the day he criticized her housekeeping. If he had, they might have faced the issue much sooner and with less pain.

Just as the paternal spouse is too protective, the maternal spouse is excessively nurturing. We will be quick to point out that some appropriate and mutual nurturing

occurs in every healthy marriage. Nurturing, like protectiveness, can enrich a marriage. However, it's again a
matter of balance. You can cross the line that turns
appropriate nurturing into unhealthy maternalism.

How can you tell when you have crossed the line? Apply
the same two tests we used for the paternal spouse. That is,
are you keeping secrets? Fred had his secret agreement that
he never shared with Virginia; only in counseling did he
acknowledge and deal with it. The second test is, would you
want your spouse to do to you what you are doing to him or
her? Would you consider the behavior maternalistic if it
were done to you?

PARENTING OUR SPOUSES

We can think of at least three reasons why people
become, or try to become, parental in their relationships
with their spouses. None of the three are consistent with
biblical principles of relating.

Work-Role Inertia

We learned the principle of inertia in elementary
physics: it is the tendency to remain in the same state. If a
body is moving, it will continue to move unless something
acts to stop it. If a body is at rest, it will remain at rest
unless something acts to get it to move.

Interpersonal inertia is the tendency to relate to
everyone in the same way, regardless of the circumstances.
In particular, some people tend to relate to family members
the way they relate to people in their work role. The movie
The Great Santini provides a perfect example. It tells the
story of a military man who ran his home and related to his
wife and children as if they were his military subordinates.

If you or your spouse work in a leadership position
where you give directives to your subordinates, you may
tend to relate to your family in the same way unless you
switch out of the work-role mode. Tom, for example, is a

successful corporate executive. He has risen to the position of vice president of production. Usually he is able to separate his work from his family life. But on a few occasions, his wife, Beth, told us, she had to remind him of the difference. "He would come home preoccupied with work. Then he would start giving commands to me, as if I was one of his assistants. For instance, one evening he even came into the kitchen and started telling me how to handle the meal. I stopped him and said, 'Wait a minute. Remember that you're not *my* vice president.' That always jars him out of it, and he's okay again. He realizes what he has been doing."

For Beth, Tom's work-role inertia was an occasional annoyance. For others, it may be a more serious problem. You can't relate to your spouse the way you relate to a child, a subordinate, a client, a customer, or a boss, and expect to have a healthy marriage. Indeed, adapting to the needs and special circumstances of different people in order to relate more effectively to all is a sound biblical principle. As Paul wrote: "I have become all things to all men so that by all possible means I might save some" (1 Cor. 9:22).

Misguided Roles

To some extent, we do for each other the kinds of things that God does for us: "Bear with each other and forgive whatever grievances you may have against one another. Forgive as the Lord forgave you" (Col. 3:13). And to some extent, spouses do for each other the kinds of things their parents did for them: as we have noted, spouses should be protective of each other, and they should nurture each other.

Yet in doing for each other what God does for us, we must not try to be God to our spouses. And in doing for each other what our parents did for us, we must not try to be parents to our spouses. Unfortunately, some Christians have misguided notions of what their roles are as husbands and wives, and they try to do for their spouses what only God or a parent could and should do.

Let's look at an example and see how Christians with differing understandings of their roles would act. Consider nurturing behavior. God nurtures us through his Holy Spirit: "But when he, the Spirit of truth, comes, he will guide you into all truth" (John 16:13). Parents, both mothers and fathers, are called to nurture their children: "Fathers, do not exasperate your children; instead, bring them up in the training and instruction of the Lord" (Eph. 6:4). And husbands and wives are to nurture each other, for nurturing is a part of Christian love (Col. 3:19; Titus 2:4).

Let's look at how a nurturing situation proved to be an ethical dilemma for Philip, a friend of ours. As a first-line manager in a small company, Philip had to deal with a subordinate who had a drinking problem. The man was an officer in Philip's church, though to Philip's knowledge no one else in the church knew of the drinking problem.

Since the drinking problem was affecting the man's performance at work, Philip had to confront him. Upper management would have supported dismissal. The man begged Philip not to fire him, pleading with him as a fellow Christian to give him another chance.

Philip now had to deal with the dilemma. How should he behave as a Christian? Would firing the man be a betrayal of the Lord who commanded us to forgive one another? Would it destroy any chances of the man's rehabilitation if he lost both his source of income and his reputation at church? On the other hand, giving the man another chance jeopardized Philip's own position; his boss would hold him responsible for the man's performance. Would it be fair to Philip's family to jeopardize his source of income? Philip even wondered if it was fair to the church to keep the man's drinking habits a secret.

Philip told his wife about his perplexity over what course of action to take. We do not know the outcome. However, let's use the situation to speculate about how his wife could have reacted. What is his wife's role in such a situation? If she was inclined to play God or to play the part of parent, she might tell him forthrightly what action to take. She wouldn't necessarily give him reasons but would expect him to do what she said anyway. If she played the role of a nurturing wife, on the other hand, she would listen carefully to Philip's story. She would work with him to identify all possible options. She would discuss with him the possible outcomes of the various options. She would explore his feelings about the options. And she would assure him of her support in whatever decision he made. If he asked, she might tell him what she would probably do under the circumstances. But the decision would be his. In this scenario, Philip's wife has been appropriately nurturing.

In other words, if you try to nurture or protect your spouse by withholding information or by ordering or expecting him or her to behave as you think best, you have a misguided understanding of your role. Marriage is not a matter of one spouse taking charge of the other but of both working together for their mutual benefit.

Self-Serving Motives

For the most part, we have implied that a spouse's motives are good in the parental approach to marriage. The spouse desires to protect, to nurture, to help. However, spouses can also act from self-serving motives. Abraham played the parental spouse to Sarah when they were about to enter Egypt, ordering her to tell the Egyptians that she was his sister. But he acknowledged that his motives were to protect himself, not Sarah: "Say you are my sister, so that I will be treated well for your sake and my life will be spared because of you" (Gen. 12:13).

Think again about the story of Fred and Virginia. Why was Fred so determined that Virginia would do things the way his mother did them? Besides idealizing his mother, Fred had another motive, one that came out only after many hours of discussion.

Fred has an older brother who is very successful in business. For a long time, at family get-togethers Fred listened in silence as his brother would talk about his business. Fred loved and admired his brother, but he also longed to do something that would show that he too had succeeded at something in a special way. Fred wanted his brother to admire him.

For Fred, attaining some kind of special success came to mean having a wife who vastly outperformed his brother's wife. In a sense, then, the two brothers were in a secret competition. If his brother's trophy was a highly successful business, Fred's trophy was Virginia. As long as Virginia measured up, Fred felt good about himself and went to family gatherings with anticipation. When Virginia failed to measure up, Fred felt that he was going to the gatherings as a loser.

GOOD-BYE PARENTS, HELLO SPOUSE

Marriage is a call to leave parents and become partners. If you or your spouse plays the role of the parental spouse, use the following statements as a daily covenant:

1. I will be your spouse, not your God or your parent.
2. I will be protective and nurturing, but not by keeping secrets from you.
3. I will be protective and nurturing, as I expect you to be with me, by listening, discussing, exploring, supporting, advising when you want me to, and by respecting your decisions.
4. Whenever I tend to be a parent rather than a partner, I want you to tell me and help me recognize my motives so that I can avoid my parenting tendencies in the future.
5. I want you to help me remember that by being partners we are fulfilling God's will for our relationship, and we will find the richness of married life that he intends for us to have.

CHAPTER 6

Family Secrets

*H*ow would you feel if the woman you thought was your mother told you on her death bed that you were adopted? How would you feel if the parents you thought were happy together and committed to each other announced one day that they were getting a divorce? How would you feel if the spouse you thought was devoted to you confessed one day to a long-term affair?

Such things happen in families. But we seldom discuss them. Husbands and wives don't mention them. Even if the children know about them (and they frequently do), they are also taught to say nothing. But eventually the secrets erupt into a serious problem. For instance, Laura and Bob had marital problems almost from the beginning of their marriage. At first Laura complained that Bob had changed into an irritable husband who spent more time with his work and hobbies than he did with her. Bob, on the other hand, complained that Laura didn't understand men in general and him in particular.

These complaints only masked the real problem. On their wedding night Laura had been "too exhausted and nervous" to have sex. Bob was willing to wait. They did consummate the marriage on the third night, but it was not satisfying for either of them. Laura loved Bob and was generally affectionate, but she became extremely tense and unresponsive when they had sex. Bob reacted by diverting his attention to other things; he spent increasingly long hours on his favorite hobby—woodworking projects.

Once we were able to help Laura and Bob openly acknowledge their problem, Laura was able to go to the root of her feelings. She explained that when she was twelve years old, a man had tried to rape her. He was frightened off before completing the rape, but the incident terrified Laura and left her with intense feelings. "I was so afraid. I thought he was going to kill me after he raped me. I was too afraid even to scream. I couldn't even talk. When I got home, I felt nervous and more angry than I've ever been in my life. I wanted to take someone and go back and find that man and kill him."

Rape victims commonly have these feelings, but Laura had never had a chance to work through them. When she came home and told her parents what had happened, her mother cried and held her, and her father muttered something about the fact that her shorts were too tight, making Laura feel as if she were to blame for the attack. The next day neither Laura's father nor her mother would talk about the rape attempt. Somehow they regarded it as an embarrassment to the family.

Laura pushed it out of her mind. But on her wedding night she found herself unable to respond to Bob with anything but a sense of horror. At the time, she didn't even understand her own feelings. She never linked them with the attempted rape until hours of counseling helped her to see that the old feelings had finally surfaced again. This time, she could work through them.

Bob was stunned when Laura told the counselor about the incident. "Why haven't you ever told me this?"

"I truly had forgotten all about it," she responded.

Fortunately, Bob and Laura were not willing to continue in an unsatisfying marriage. If they had, the secret that Laura's family had kept would have contaminated their marriage, and that would be damaging to any children they have. That's why family secrets are so insidious. They can keep on harming people's relationships for generations.

THE NATURE OF FAMILY SECRETS

What kinds of family experiences might a couple try to keep secret? As Laura and Bob illustrate, a horrendous incident like rape or attempted rape is one thing. Counselors report quite a few others, including:

- Excessive drinking or drug abuse
- Adopting a child or having a child by artificial insemination
- Incest
- Rape
- Having a child as a result of incest or rape
- Getting married because the woman is pregnant
- Having an affair
- Getting an abortion
- Physical and/or emotional abuse
- Financial problems
- Learning disabilities
- Unethical or illegal activities
- Chronic or terminal disease.

You are probably not surprised that couples would want to keep some of these things secret. You may wonder, however, at a few of the items in this list (which is not at all complete). For example, why do people try to keep a secret of a child's learning disability or a family member's terminal disease? And if they do, aren't people cutting themselves off from getting important and needed help? The answer is yes. But despite the negative consequences, some couples try to maintain the secret.

The point is, people find innumerable reasons to keep secrets, and not all of them are the skeleton-in-the-closet type of secrets. Yet all family secrets share at least one thing in common: the attempt to keep secrets has negative consequences for family members. Refusing to acknowledge a child's learning disability or a family member's alcohol problem or a parent's abuse obviously means that one or more family members are not getting the help they need. It also means that a husband and wife are colluding in an unhealthy refusal to face reality. In a sense, to refuse to face reality is to fail to accept the sufficiency of God's grace for any of life's problems. Eventually, reality catches up to us, and we suffer.

In facing one aspect of the reality of her life, Laura had to face another aspect: how she would relate to her parents. She is angry and hurt that their refusal to help her work through the pain of the attempted rape led to serious personal and marital problems for her. Not only must she work through her feelings about the incident, but she also faces the uncertainty and anguish of how to deal with her parents. Family secrets don't stay buried; they only increase the pain of traumatic experiences.

WHY KEEP THE SECRET?

In view of the negative consequences, why do people try to maintain family secrets? In a sense, the answer is simple: they expect to be better off in some way by keeping the secret. Even if they realize that secrets have brought negative consequences to others, they believe that they themselves will benefit. What are those benefits?

Maintaining Respectability

One of the major reasons that Christians get caught up in family secrets is the desire to maintain respectability. After all, isn't it better for our witness if we are free of such things as drug and alcohol problems, incest, adultery, and even chronic health problems? Isn't it important that we show the world how God can enable us to be righteous, healthy, satisfied people?

The problem with answering yes to such questions is that it does no good to present the world with a façade of respectability. In fact, it is worse than "no good"; it is an exercise in a deception that will only increase the world's contempt for the name of Jesus Christ.

Let's look at the situation in a different way. Is it better to pretend that a problem doesn't exist or to acknowledge it and ask for the help of God's people to overcome it? The Bible does not try to hide people's shortcomings and struggles. Think, for example, of Paul's letters to the various churches. We know about such things as the divisions and immorality in the Corinthian church and the conflict between Euodia and Syntyche at Philippi and the idle, busybodies at Thessalonica because Paul realized that it is important to face our sins rather than to maintain a façade of respectability. Only when we face our sins can we grow in the grace and knowledge and likeness of Jesus Christ.

Avoiding Negative Consequences

A second apparent benefit in keeping family secrets is to avoid the negative consequences of acknowledgment and exposure. For instance, if you have a serious shortcoming and acknowledge the situation, will it destroy your marriage and your family? Recall Becky's story, which we described in chapter 2. One of the main reasons that Becky didn't confront her father's incestuous attacks was her fear that the family would completely fall apart if she did.

We also fear that if others find out about the secret, they will despise us, or at the very least think less of us. For example, what if you are having marital problems and people in your church find out? Will they pray for you and try to help you, or will they label you as a poor Christian?

Such concerns are not groundless. A woman whose marriage broke up told us, "I was a Sunday-school teacher for years. I kept teaching even when my marriage started going downhill. But when my husband filed for divorce, I was too distraught to keep preparing lessons. I resigned. A year after my divorce, I felt my life was coming back together, and I was eager to get back into church work again. But they wouldn't allow me to teach Sunday school any more. According to them, a divorced woman was not a proper role model for children."

Such things can happen. On the other hand, we have heard countless stories of people who received support from their church through all kinds of crises. Many churches have Alcoholics Anonymous groups for alcoholics, Al-Anon groups for the spouses of alcoholics, twelve-step groups for people with various kinds of problematic backgrounds, singles groups that support the divorced as well as the widowed and never-married, and so on. In other words, while Christians who choose to confront rather than try to maintain a family secret may encounter rejection, it is more likely that they will encounter support and understanding.

Whether we try to keep the secrets or try to confront them, we take risks. Either choice brings some negative consequences. But the potential for good is stronger if we are willing to expose the secrets and trust God's wisdom, grace, and forgiveness to bring us into greater wholeness.

Remaining Loyal

A third apparent benefit of keeping a family secret is maintaining loyalty. Keeping the secret is a way of saying, "We stick together. We help and protect each other."

To be sure, loyalty is good. However, loyalty can also be misguided, as illustrated by an interesting Old Testament story. The event occurred when David and his men were fighting the Philistines. At the time, the Philistines were in control of Bethlehem. "David longed for water and said, 'Oh, that someone would get me a drink of water from the well near the gate of Bethlehem!'" (2 Sam. 23:15). Three of his strong men heard him, broke through the Philistine lines, and brought the water back to David. But he then refused to drink it, pouring it out as an offering to God instead. "'Far be it from me, O Lord, to do this!' he said. 'Is it not the blood of men who went at the risk of their lives?'" (2 Sam. 23:17).

In other words, the men had acted loyally, eager to serve the needs of their leader. Yet it was a misguided loyalty; David needed them more than he needed the water from Bethlehem's well. Similarly, it is a misguided kind of family loyalty that seeks to protect those engaged in destructive behavior. In such circumstances, your family needs your help, not your defense. You are not expressing loyalty to others when you ignore or defend their troubled behavior. You are only colluding with them in a situation that is certain to be detrimental to both of you.

For example, Nora struggled for years to help her husband, Vern, a deacon in the church. Vern had periods of depression when he doubted his faith and felt like a spiritual fraud. Nora would enlist the aid of their child, Sonny, to "help father feel better." Sonny grew up feeling responsible for his father's well-being, and when Vern died Sonny went through a period of deep guilt and depression. Nora regrets now that she did not urge Vern to get professional help: "We didn't want to embarrass him, so I told Sonny we must never tell anyone else." She knows now that Sonny paid a price for their family secret. She thought she was being loyal to Vern; rather, she was building trouble for her son.

SECRET FROM WHOM?

One way to categorize family secrets is to ask from whom we are trying to keep the secret. We can then identify three types of family secrets: we-them secrets, house-divided secrets, and collective-denial secrets. Let's look at each type.

We-Them Secrets

The first type involves secrets that are known in the family but kept from all outsiders. "We" know; "they" don't, and must not. This was the kind of secret that Ananias and Sapphira attempted to keep, agreeing together to pretend to give all the proceeds of a land sale to the church while withholding some for themselves (Acts 5:1–2).

This is the kind of secret that some of our acquaintances kept for years while they were near bankruptcy. The man's business faltered, but they did not alter their living pattern. For nearly two years, people at their church believed them to be as financially successful as they had been in the early years of the man's business. Only when they were forced to sell their house and other properties did others learn of their problems. Unfortunately, they then had to deal not only with their continuing financial woes but also with the pain of confronting the past two years of deception.

We-them secrets are likely to be concerned with maintaining the appearance of respectability. For some Christians, respectability simply means avoiding any kind of gross immorality. For others, however, it may mean something even more. Consider Richard, a professional man in his forties. Richard and his wife, Marlene, have three children, ranging in age from six to eleven. Richard and his family came to our community when his youngest child was only a few months old. For nearly six years Richard insisted that his family keep a secret from their friends at church: the secret was that their three children were adopted. Why should that be a secret? Richard told us the reason. "When I first discovered that I was sterile, I was shattered. I felt less of a man. What kind of man would be unable to father children? I felt that God had cheated me out of something that was really important to me. It wasn't just my manhood, of course. I always loved children and always wanted them. So I began to pray that he would correct the condition. I thought that if he could give Abraham and Sarah a child in their old age, he could surely heal my sterility.

"Nothing happened. The whole thing was a spiritual and emotional disaster for me. I got through it with my wife's help, and we adopted our three children. But when we moved here, I saw the chance to become what I had wanted to be in the first place—a man who had fathered children."

But the children all knew they were adopted, and one of them gave the secret away when a friend asked why she didn't look like her mother or father. Richard was embarrassed as he acknowledged what he had done. His attempt to gain what he regarded as greater respectability resulted in, at least temporarily, a loss of respectability.

House-Divided Secrets

In a second type of family secret, some family members keep the secret from other family members. The family is a house divided against itself. A classic instance of this kind of deception was the deception Rebecca and Jacob practiced on Isaac and Esau (Gen. 27). Rebecca conspired with Jacob to get the blessing of the blind Isaac, a blessing that should have gone to Esau, the firstborn. Ultimately, God used the situation for good. Yet in the short run, the net effect was that Rebecca practiced deception, Isaac was deceived, Esau was cheated and embittered, and Jacob learned how to be a trickster.

In the house-divided secret, one spouse may enlist the help of other family members to maintain the secret. For example, Joan is a professional woman who had a brief extra-marital affair with a colleague. Her husband, Warren, never knew about it. Joan deeply regrets the affair and has been faithful to Warren ever since.

Joan regrets something else, however. One day while she was having lunch with the colleague, Joan's sister-in-law arrived at the lunch table only to find the two of them holding hands. Joan's sister-in-law had called Joan's place of work, found out where Joan was having lunch, and had decided to surprise her by showing up unannounced.

Joan was more than surprised. She was horrified. Her sister-in-law was angry and disappointed, but she agreed to say nothing. However, Joan is still struggling with what she has done. "I know the secret is safe as far as Warren is concerned, but I also know that I have lost something both with Warren and with my sister-in-law. It's ironic, isn't it? I thought I was protecting my marriage by not telling Warren. But I still feel so guilty that I can't relate to him as I once did. I thought that as long as he doesn't know, he'll feel the same about me. I never realized that as long as I do know, I can't feel the same about myself or us. It's almost as if I'm still deceiving him by not telling him. And I'm forcing my sister-in-law to join me in the lie."

We don't know how Joan ultimately will resolve her problem. She is caught between a fear of losing Warren if she tells him and the agony of ongoing guilt if she doesn't. And her situation is compounded by another thought: "I should have confessed and asked for Warren's forgiveness. Now I'm afraid that if I tell him, he'll say that he could have accepted it if I had told him right away. I'm also concerned that if I tell him that his sister discovered my secret, he'll say that I ended the affair only because I was discovered."

It's too bad that Joan sees things so clearly only in retrospect. She makes an important point that anyone tempted to engage in this kind of family secret should recognize: not only will the secret itself be detrimental to the marriage relationship, but bringing other family members in to help maintain the secret only adds to the complexity and difficulty of finally resolving it.

Collective-Denial Secrets

In the third type of family secret, some or all the family members know the family secret, but they pretend they don't know. This, of course, is denial. It is collective denial. It is the explicit or tacit agreement of family members to act as if something doesn't exist.

This type of secret may have occurred in King David's family. One of David's sons, Amnon, fell in love with one of David's daughters, Tamar. Amnon feigned illness to get Tamar to come to him, then he raped her. She let her brother Absalom know of the rape, and David found out about it and was "furious" (2 Sam. 13:21). However, Absalom said nothing to Amnon. Apparently David said nothing more either. Two years later Absalom had Amnon killed (2 Sam. 13:23–29). What was going on during those two years? It would seem that the family was maintaining a secret by each one acting as if the rape had never occurred. Like all family secrets, however, this one finally ended in tragedy.

This third type of family secret is common in cases of incest. In the presence of outsiders and each other, the family members act as if they are perfectly normal. The incestuous relationship is never mentioned, and no one acts as if it is occurring. Again recall the story of Becky in chapter 2. She gave in to her father's demands precisely to maintain some kind of normalcy in her family.

This type of secret is also common in families with an alcoholic. The nonalcoholic spouse may protect the alcoholic spouse (and, in effect, maintain the alcoholism) by refusing to admit the problem either to children or to outsiders.

Other kinds of problems may also be handled through collective denial. One of the strangest divorces we have known involved Bert and April, now in their fifties. They were divorced ten years ago. April told us what sounds like an almost unbelievable case of collective denial, a denial that involved just the two of them since they have no children. "Our honeymoon period didn't last very long. We had problems almost from the beginning. The funny thing is that we never argued or fought about things. He did many things that annoyed me, but I just ignored them. Like his habit of hogging the newspaper in the morning. And the way he never picked up his clothes. I would get irked, but I never said anything. Besides, I got busy with my career, so we didn't have a whole lot of time together, and I wasn't spending that much time in the house.

"I'm sure I did things that annoyed him too. At least he seemed to withdraw from me more and more. We stopped having sex altogether. At first that bothered me. But I got used to it, and as long as I was busy, I didn't mind.

"After fifteen years of marriage, Bert unexpectedly told me he wanted a divorce. I said okay, so we separated. But we never talked about it. We never talked about what went wrong. We never talked about why either of us was unhappy with the other. We just quietly left the marriage."

During the fifteen years Bert and April were married, they denied what was happening not only to each other but also to outsiders. Their friends had no hint that anything was wrong. April recalls, "Some of my friends at work were really shocked when I told them I was getting divorced. They didn't realize that anything was wrong between Bert and me. Some of them have met Bert at parties, and they thought he seemed like a contented husband."

To this day, April shrugs her shoulders and says she still doesn't have any clear understanding about what happened in her marriage or why she and Bert never talked about their problems. However, one thing seems clear to her: through collective denial, she and Bert lost any chance they might have for building a meaningful relationship together.

THE ULTIMATE EXAMPLE

April and Bert's experience may seem extreme. However, we have one that is even more extreme, an example that will show not only the lengths to which people will go to maintain a secret but also the destructive consequences of such a secret. The example also underscores our earlier point that family secrets can create damage throughout several generations.

George is a retired engineer in his early sixties. He is a lay preacher in his church, has many friends, and keeps busy in a variety of community activities. George also has a troubled relationship with his mother, Esther. Throughout his life, he has been at odds with his mother: they disagreed about his schoolwork, his relationships with women (he never married), and how often he makes contact with her (they live in different states).

George recently received a letter from a lifelong friend of his mother. The letter revealed a secret that George's mother had kept from him all his life. The letter helped explain why George had spent the first seven years of his life in an orphanage, where his mother had sent him shortly after he was born. It helped explain why his mother had refused to tell him anything about the father he had never known. At least he *thought* he had never known him. It turned out, however, that the man George knew as his grandfather was also his father. George was born as a result of incest.

Thus the story really begins with Esther's parents and their marriage. We didn't know the parents, but Esther told us some things about them. Her father was a banker, and her mother was a stay-at-home mother. Esther, their only child, was a teenager when the incest occurred. When Esther tried to talk to her mother about the incest, however, her mother grew intensely angry and told her never to speak in such a way about her father.

Esther was perplexed by her mother's reaction. She began to watch her parents more closely and soon realized that they showed no affection toward each other. At one point she told us that she had decided that if what she saw in her parents was all that marriage was about, she wanted no part of it.

To outsiders, of course, her parents seemed to be a normal couple. In fact, her father was a highly respected member of the community. Esther realized that without her mother's support, no one would believe what her father had done. Collective denial had done its work well and had claimed Esther as a victim.

To have someone believe her was important to Esther because she got pregnant. She was unable to support a child, and her father would not acknowledge that the child was his. She was forced to put her son, George, into an orphanage until she eventually found work and was able to support him. When she brought him to live with her, he wondered about his father. But she either ignored his queries or told him that his father was no longer around. George finally stopped asking.

Because of the incest, Esther never married. She could not relate romantically to men. And because of the incest, Esther struggled with her feelings about her son. As George grew, some of his mannerisms reminded her of her father. She found herself critical of George with an intensity that she could not control. Clearly, she was still lashing out at her father.

When George went away to college, he left home for good. Eventually, he moved to another state. Esther loved her son and wanted him to keep in close touch with her. But he was also a constant reminder of her abusive father. She found herself struggling with ambivalent feelings, wanting George and resenting him.

George also had ambivalent feelings. He loved his mother, but he could never understand her continual criticism of him. He wanted to be close to her but found that he could not be in her presence for a long time without becoming thoroughly frustrated and angry.

The struggle went on for nearly sixty years! Throughout this time, Esther confided in a childhood friend, but she told no one else. Finally, George wrote his mother a letter in which he said that he loved her but simply could not cope with her demands and complaints. He would no longer come to see her or call her or talk to her on the telephone, he wrote, unless she could change her behavior toward him. He had reached a point of total frustration with their relationship.

Esther immediately called her friend and read the letter to her. For years, the friend had urged Esther to tell George the truth about his father. Now, the friend told Esther, it was imperative that George know the truth or Esther would lose him. Esther said she didn't have the strength to tell George. The friend offered to write him a letter and tell him. Esther agreed.

George was only mildly stunned when he got the letter. For some years, he had suspected that the root of his troubles with his mother was that her father was also his father. The letter confirmed his suspicion. But it also opened up the possibility of rebuilding the relationship with his mother. After sixty years of anguish, George and Esther are finally beginning to relate to each other in a new and constructive way.

To be fair, we must recognize that incest is a much more open topic of discussion than it was when Esther was victimized. Still, the tragedy of Esther's family secret was that she allowed her relationship with her son to be so distorted and disturbing for so many years because she could not bear to tell him the truth about his father.

George and his mother have lost years of potentially rich experiences together. They may never have the intimate relationship that mothers and sons desire. However, they have broken through the secret and are working on changing their relationship. But they both continue to mourn their loss. Perhaps as well as anyone we know, they are acutely aware of the destructiveness of family secrets.

WHAT IF SOMEONE FINDS OUT?

The thing that perpetuates family secrets is believing that people must not find out the truth, that the truth would be destructive. Let's explore the painful question, What if someone finds out? What will happen?

Let's go back to Esther and George for a moment. Esther's friend received a letter in return from George. In it, he told her that he was very grateful for her letter and for the truth. He acknowledged that he had suspected the truth for a number of years but was extremely relieved to know for certain. She, he wrote, was responsible for giving him and his mother a chance to have something of a normal relationship for whatever years they had left together.

In essence, George felt liberated. And this is usually what happens when the secret is finally out. People feel a sense of release, of freedom to begin a new and better kind of life. A therapist has likened family secrets to having an elephant in the living room. What a relief it is to get the elephant out!

Now getting the elephant out doesn't mean taking out an ad in your local newspaper and publicly announcing the secret. Yet if you have been haunted by a family secret, if you are weary of the struggle, and if you are eager to put your family on a more solid Christian basis, it's time to tell someone about the secret. That someone may be other members of the family if you've been involved in a house-divided or collective-denial secret. Eventually, it may be a pastor or counselor.

Who it is that needs to find out depends on the kind of secret you have. In the case of Esther and George, for instance, it was necessary for George to find out and then necessary for each of them to talk with a counselor as they began to work on their relationship.

In other cases, it may be necessary for a larger number of people to find out the secret. If you have deceived people to keep a family secret, you need to confess your deception and ask for forgiveness. If people have been hurt because of your family secret, you need to right as many wrongs as you can. Some of this may be painful. However, it is also liberating because it is an effort to be thoroughly Christian in all your relationships. Unquestionably, it is the beginning of your healing.

Jani and Tim illustrate the liberation of owning up to a family secret. Married eight years, they are both officers at their church. In their sixth year of marriage, they went through a difficult time. It was clear that their relationship was strained.

Then, at a deacon's meeting, Jani asked for some time on the agenda. She told her story. When Jani was twelve, her father announced to her mother that he was a homosexual and that he wanted a divorce. Jani maintained contact with her father and loves him as her father. But she was too embarrassed for anyone at church to know about him. She made Tim promise to say nothing.

Tim kept his promise. But he has strong feelings about

homosexuality, and when he would express his feelings at church or when they were with church friends, Jani was afraid he would let their secret slip. When they got home, Jani would berate him and insist that he needed to be more careful. He resented her lack of trust in him and insisted that he had the right to speak about the issue. Because they were heavily involved in church activities, Jani's tension mounted. Their marriage suffered.

Finally, after much prayer and discussion, Jani announced to Tim that she believed she had been wrong to keep her father's homosexuality a secret. "I can't help what he is," she said. "And surely no one can tell me to stop loving my own father. I think it's time we tell people." Tim agreed, and Jani told her story at the deacon's meeting. She got nothing but understanding and support. And without the burden of trying to maintain the secret, her relationship with Tim improved immediately.

What if someone finds out? It will probably be the most liberating experience you have had in a long time.

Part II
The High Cost of Dishonesty

A man reaps what he sows.
GALATIANS 6:7

CHAPTER 7

The Webs We Weave: Seven Things You Can Do Without

Shakespeare's *Measure for Measure* is set at a time when a law forbade any man to live with a woman who was not his wife. The penalty for breaking the law was death. However, the duke who reigned over the city was a mild man who would not enforce the law. As a result, many young people lived together without being married, and many parents of young women complained bitterly to the duke.

The duke realized he had to do something to save the institution of marriage. He decided to go away for a time and appoint someone else to be in charge, someone who would enforce the law. The duke chose Angelo, a man with a reputation for living a very strict life. About the time that Angelo took over as lord deputy, a young man named Claudio persuaded a young woman to leave her parents and live with him.

Angelo, enforcing the law, commanded Claudio to be imprisoned and then to be beheaded. Claudio's sister, Isabel, went to Angelo to beg him to spare her brother. Angelo said he could not. But as she spoke, Angelo was greatly stirred by her beauty. Finally, Angelo tried to seduce her and told her that he would spare Claudio if she would surrender to his desires. Isabel was outraged that he should propose to her the very thing for which he had condemned her brother to death. He reminded her, however, that no one would believe her if she revealed his proposition, for he had a sterling reputation. He pressed her to submit. In the end, through a variety of developments, Angelo does not get his way.

Shakespeare's character depicts a very common human trait. Angelo represents all people who believe that the rules do not apply to them, that they do not suffer the consequences of breaking the rules.

The apostle Paul, on the other hand, reminds us that a person "reaps what he sows" (Gal. 6:7). None of us can break the rules with impunity. And one of the rules of marriage and family life is that dishonesty causes destructive consequences. Family researchers have found that dishonesty is associated with lower marital satisfaction. There are quite a few additional consequences, however, a number of which we have mentioned in previous chapters. Here, we want to explore seven different consequences.

CONSEQUENCE 1: LOSS OF INTIMACY

Dishonesty always involves some loss of intimacy. The way we become intimate with someone is to share our feelings, our thoughts, our aspirations, our fears. Of course, no one shares everything with another person. There is a difference, however, between things not shared and things deliberately withheld to deceive.

Recall the story of Jan and David, whom we discussed in chapter 2. Jan is the professional woman who withholds her clothing purchases from David. We pointed out that such dishonesty detracts from intimacy. But how? Jan, as we noted, doesn't think that her secret is harmful; in fact, she thinks she is doing her marriage a service by avoiding arguments over the money she spends on clothes. But when we probed the issue with Jan, it was clear that the level of intimacy in their marriage suffered as a result of her secrets.

Jan told us about a time when she was wearing a particularly "stunning" new outfit. It was one of those rare occasions when David noticed. He mentioned that he didn't recall seeing the suit before. Jan laughed, kissed him, and reminded him that he never noticed what she wore and would not recognize a new suit from one that was five years old. "And how did he react to that?" we asked. Jan said he was perfectly satisfied, which proved her point that she is not damaging her marriage in any way.

We were not convinced. We pursued the issue: "So David never raised the issue again?"

"No."

"Why do you think he doesn't notice what you wear? He seems to be a generally observant guy."

"He is. But he's usually rushing around in the morning, getting ready for work himself. And he seldom gets home from work before I do."

"But you have a lot of social engagements because of your work. Doesn't he notice what you wear then?"

"Oh, David rarely goes with me. I was a little worried about that myself, but I decided that he would enjoy himself more doing something else. That's easier on me. When he does go with me, I'm careful not to wear something new. But most of the time, I just tell him when I have an engagement, and he plans on doing something with his friends. And I let it go at that."

Further discussion brought out the fact that Jan and David spend very little leisure time together—a practice that resulted from Jan's desire to cover up her purchases. Now it has become a way of life. Jan frequently does things with business associates and friends while David plays tennis or attends movies with his friends. Since shared leisure activities are an important part of intimacy, their intimacy is clearly suffering at this point. Jan's secret turns out to be not as benign or helpful as she insists. Even in the short term, it is clear to us that it is damaging to their intimacy.

And in the long term, it could be disastrous as their lives tend increasingly to go off in different directions.

Dishonesty also leads to a loss of intimacy with God. When David repented of his adulterous affair with Bathsheba, he cried out in anguish to God: "Against you, you only, have I sinned and done what is evil in your sight" (Ps. 51:4). David had taken advantage of Bathsheba and had caused her husband to be killed in a vain effort to hide his own sin. Yet he says that his sin was against God. Indeed, all sin is against God. When we are dishonest with another person, we are dishonest with God.

Moreover, as a result of his sin, David experienced a loss of intimacy with God, for he pleaded: "Restore to me the joy of your salvation and grant me a willing spirit, to sustain me" (Ps. 51:12). When we are dishonest with another person, we are dishonest with God. When we are dishonest with God, we experience a loss of intimacy with him.

Intimacy with God and with others is a crucial part of our well-being. This first consequence of dishonesty, therefore, strikes at the heart of our spiritual and emotional health.

CONSEQUENCE 2: STUNTED GROWTH

"I have come," Jesus said, "that they may have life, and have it to the full" (John 10:10). That strikes a responsive note in everyone: we all want to do more than merely exist; we want to live life to the full. Among other things, a full life demands growth.

The importance of growth is illustrated by the experience of a writer who some years ago spent a number of weeks on a South Pacific island. Like many people, the writer went with the idea that an earthly paradise is a place where one can enjoy sunshine and leisure each day and be free from all the cares that afflict us in modern society.

When the writer got to the island, he found the natives very friendly. The sun shone every day, and he found little work to do. But one day the writer reflected on his experiences and realized something that startled him: he was incredibly bored! In the midst of a growing discontent, he discovered some old American magazines. As he read through them, he realized that the people he was reading about were engaged with life, while he was simply vegetating and growing increasingly restless. Shortly thereafter, he gladly left his "paradise" and returned to his home. He realized that a paradise somehow disconnected from the ferment of human life is an illusion.

We do not grow without being engaged with life, and we do not experience life deeply without growing. What's the use of having a long life, Thomas à Kempis wrote in his famous *Imitation of Christ*, if you can't show improvement in it? In other words, a long life without growth is only an extended exercise in triviality. To live is to grow. To grow is to live. The Bible underscores the point by frequently portraying the godly life as one of growth. And Peter's last words to us are: "But grow in the grace and knowledge of our Lord and Savior Jesus Christ. To him be glory both now and forever! Amen" (2 Peter 3:18).

Thus, the second consequence of dishonesty—stunted growth—is also critical to our well-being. Dishonesty stunts the growth in the relationship. We tend to think of growth as something involving the individual, but relationships also need to grow—in intimacy, in satisfaction, in understanding of each other, in mutually adapting to each other's needs, and so on.

Dishonesty puts the brakes on a couple's growth. If, for instance, a part of growing as a couple is an increased understanding of each other, that growth cannot happen if one person is withholding something from the other. More than one person has come to us after years of marriage and said, "I sometimes feel as if I don't even know my husband [or wife]." Frequently it turns out that the perplexity has come about because the other person has not been open and honest about some feeling or behavior. The relationship has become stagnant instead of continuing to grow to higher levels of fulfillment because one of the spouses is to some extent insulated from the other by dishonesty.

CONSEQUENCE 3: THE WEB SYNDROME

The old line about the tangled web we weave when we set out to deceive is well illustrated by David's affair with Bathsheba. Adultery led to further efforts to deceive Uriah, Bathsheba's husband, and finally to murder Uriah. While the webs we weave with dishonesty are not likely to lead to something as extreme as murder, they probably will become increasingly complex and increasingly filled with additional deceit.

Recall the discussion in chapter 2 of Jan and David's secret-compartment marriage. For a long time, Jan has secretly spent money on clothing she feels she needs in her career. On at least one occasion, Jan acknowledges her practice has led her to engage in further deceit, which has made her feel quite uncomfortable. "I remember that it was just after Christmas. David and I had gone to some friends' home for dinner. I was wearing a new dress that I had bought a few weeks before. David, as usual, paid no attention. But one of the women commented on how chic it was, noted that it was new, and asked where I had gotten it.

"Out of the corner of my eye, I saw David look up and stare at the dress. I could tell that he was thinking he hadn't seen it before. I really felt bad about it later, but I was on the spot and just blurted out that one of my close friends at work had given it to me for Christmas. Of course, that was hard to believe. David has no sense of how much women's clothes cost, so he seemed satisfied. But the woman who had asked me about the dress was amazed that a friend would have given me such an expensive present. Later on, she pursued the topic with me. So I fabricated this whole story about a friend who was grateful because I had helped save her job. I nearly felt sick when I got home that night. I was so ashamed."

That incident nearly caused Jan to take our counsel

and confront David with the situation. So far, however, she still hasn't done so. And eventually, she will undoubtedly find herself in other situations where she will have to compound the dishonesty about her clothing purchases with further deceit.

Some people who have been dishonest in their marriage find that when they try to rectify the situation, the webs they have woven make their efforts agonizingly difficult. A woman confessed to us that she told her husband she had to go out of town on short business trips. She stayed with the man with whom she was having an affair. When she talked with us, she was breaking off the affair. She had asked for God's forgiveness and was eager once again to be faithful to her husband. Yet the situation was still complicated. She had decided, at least for the time being, not to tell her husband about the affair: "He would be shattered, and I'm afraid it might wreck our marriage. But it's going to be difficult to know how to explain that I suddenly no longer have to go out of town on work. I don't want to ever lie to him again. What should I do?"

The webs we weave in dishonest relationships can become so perplexingly tangled that only the grace and power of God can enable us to get out of them. Even then, we can't escape without going through anguish. Blessed are those who never even begin to weave such webs.

CONSEQUENCE 4: DIMINISHED TRUST

In our study of long-term, successful marriages, we found that trust was an important part of spouses feeling secure in the relationship. Mutual trust provides each spouse with security; it means that the spouse wastes little energy on jealousy, suspicion, and behavior aimed at getting reassurance from the other.

When trust declines or is lacking, a relationship deteriorates and typically sinks into ongoing conflict. For instance, if you don't trust your spouse, if you don't have a firm sense that your spouse is honest, supportive, and loyal, you will probably find yourself continually challenging your spouse on a variety of issues. When one spouse doesn't trust the other, all kinds of behavior become suspect. Such things as being late, going somewhere alone, spending time with a friend of the opposite sex, and criticizing the spouse's behavior all become suspect when there is no trust.

For example, a husband may say to his wife: "That color of red doesn't look very good on you." When trust exists, the wife will take that to be a helpful observation. When trust is weak, the wife might translate the statement to mean: "He's criticizing me. He finds other women more attractive. He really doesn't like me anymore."

Clearly, mutual trust is essential to a healthy marriage. It should be equally clear that dishonesty strikes a blow at mutual trust. Obviously, trust will suffer when the dishonesty is discovered. We have repeatedly found people struggling to be able to trust again after a spouse has confessed some kind of dishonesty and pledged to be honest in the future. "I think I've forgiven him," as one woman put it, "but I still find myself being suspicious." A trust that is broken is very difficult to restore completely.

Trust can be lost even when the dishonesty hasn't yet been discovered. Dishonest behavior tends to generate suspicion in others because few of us can act dishonestly and still appear to be perfectly honest. An observant spouse is likely to pick up some cues that something is amiss.

An example of loss of trust occurred when Wendy was victimized by a secret marital agreement. Wendy's husband, Ron, expected her to check with him before making any plans either for herself or for the two of them. Ron's father was a retired military officer. Ron's mother had always acceded to his father's wishes just as if she were one of his subordinates. Among other things, to make sure that what she did was acceptable, Ron's mother checked with him before planning her own day. Ron grew up thinking that it was normal and proper for a wife to talk with her husband before making any plans.

Wendy, on the other hand, had grown up in a more

typical home. Her mother and father had their own activities each day. For things that involved both of them, they talked and planned together. But each would, at times, tentatively agree to do something that involved the other as well. It never occurred to Wendy to get Ron's approval before making any plans.

For a time, Wendy and Ron had small arguments when she would do something that he hadn't known about in advance. A typical argument went like this:

Wendy: "Look what I found at the store today (showing him a scarf she had purchased)."

Ron: "Why did you go shopping today?"

Wendy: "What do you mean why? Because I needed to, that's why."

Ron: "You never told me you were going shopping."

Wendy: "Do I need to tell you? What do you think I'm doing, meeting another guy or something?"

Ron: "I never said that. Why do you bring it up?"

When Wendy and Ron came to counseling, these kinds of arguments had become a way of life, and their mutual trust had eroded considerably. Ron had begun to think that Wendy might be cheating on him. Wendy was appalled by his suspicions and his constant demand to know in advance what she was doing each day.

It was only in counseling that Ron realized the role his parents played in his expectations. And fortunately he was able to change. Even so, it took time for the spouses to restore their trust in each other. Wendy had been deeply hurt that Ron had suspected her of infidelity. Ron was deeply hurt that Wendy didn't want to tell him everything that she did. Each felt betrayed to some extent by the other. Each felt the erosion of trust long before they were aware of the secret expectations that were sabotaging their relationship. Ron and Wendy learned by bitter experience that mutual trust is crucial but also fragile and that it can quickly be lost in a dishonest marriage.

CONSEQUENCE 5: UNLEARNED PROBLEM-SOLVING SKILLS

A fundamental educational rule is that we learn by doing. If you want to gain skill in anything, you need to practice it. One of the skills you need for a satisfying marriage is the ability to solve problems. Someone has said that even if marriages are made in heaven, the details have to be worked out on earth. In other words, every marriage will have to confront an ongoing set of problems, from setting up an acceptable division of labor in the home to deciding how to budget the money to coming to agreement on how to discipline children, and so on.

A man in a long-term marriage told us that a major difficulty for young couples today is that they are too quick to give up because of the ongoing problems. "My wife and I worked our way through problems that today we might walk away from. Our marriage is firm and filled with respect and love, and it took time and work. But by contemporary standards for marriage, we should never have survived as a couple. We probably would have separated during our first year together. I'm glad we didn't. I can't emphasize this too strongly. I have two children who divorced. They are still searching for a magical something that isn't obtainable in the real world. Marriage grows through working out problems and going on. Our marriage has been developing for forty years, and we are still learning."

Many problems have to be solved over and over. For example, we have known many couples who had an acceptable division of labor in the home early on in their marriage and who had to work out a new agreement when the wife entered the labor force after the children were in school.

You can't avoid problems in marriage, but you can respond to them in either helpful or destructive ways. Dishonesty is a destructive attempt to deal with some problematic issue, and typically dishonesty attempts to resolve the issue by avoiding the work of problem solving. In the case of Jan and David, for example, rather than confront

David and work with him on an acceptable compromise, Jan chose to avoid the work of problem solving by deceiving her spouse.

Of course, this means that, besides the other consequences, Jan deprived herself of an opportunity to practice and sharpen her problem-solving skills. She doesn't feel that she lacks those skills. She insists that she and David are capable of working out every other issue except this one. Yet Jan and David have not faced any other issue on which they have such strong disagreement. When they do, will she confront it, or will she again try the seemingly easier way of deceit?

CONSEQUENCE 6: FLAWED WITNESS

People who are sexually immoral, thieves, greedy, drunkards, slanderers, or swindlers, Paul wrote to the Corinthians, will not inherit the kingdom of God. Then he reminded them: "And that is what some of you were. But you were washed, you were sanctified, you were justified in the name of the Lord Jesus Christ and by the Spirit of our God" (1 Cor. 6:11).

This character transformation that Paul described to the Corinthians has always been a crucial part of the Christian witness. Those concerned about maintaining the integrity of that witness, therefore, should be careful not to fall prey to dishonesty in marriage. What does it say about the transforming power of Christ if a Christian can't be forthright and open in dealing with his or her spouse?

To return to the case of Jan and David, again, Jan has shared her secret with only a few others, mainly her close female friends. But among those female friends is one who is not a Christian. And she doesn't show any interest in becoming a Christian. Unfortunately, Jan can have little impact on her as long as her friend is aware of Jan's deceit.

The non-Christian friend has also engaged in deception with her husband and has shared that with Jan. Jan's closest friends have few secrets among them. It no doubt gives Jan's non-Christian friend great comfort to know a professed Christian who behaves the same way she does. And we can imagine the friend saying to someone who tried to talk to her about Christ, "I don't see any difference between the way I live and the way my Christian friends live."

To look at the other side of the coin, if dishonesty flaws our witness, honesty can sharpen it. Sometimes non-Christians are amazed when they see a marriage in which two people openly and honestly work together to build a stable and satisfying union. Sam and Lila are one such couple. They have been married for twelve years. Lila recalled a time when she had an opportunity to witness to her faith by talking about her marital relationship. "I was talking with a non-Christian about the problems of marriage. This person had overspent her budget the past month and was wondering how she was going to cope with it. 'I've done that a lot,' I told her, trying to reassure her that it wasn't a disaster. 'Maybe you can just juggle some things around next month.'

"'But,' she said, 'how did you keep your husband from finding out about it?'

"For a moment I was stunned into silence. Then I told her it didn't even occur to me to try. My husband and I always are honest with each other, and we work together on those kinds of problems. She only sighed and said how lucky I was, but she couldn't do that. Then I was able to point out that as a Christian couple, we had learned long ago the importance of being honest and trusting each other and helping each other deal with those kinds of difficulties."

Lila has not seen the woman since the episode. However, she remembers that the woman looked "really impressed" when she told her how her Christian faith had helped her fashion an honest marriage. Honest marriages are rare. Those who have them bear an important witness to the power of God in their lives.

CONSEQUENCE 7: VIOLATING LOVE

Finally, dishonesty is a violation of love. When we marry, we promise to love and honor one another. "Love must be sincere," wrote Paul (Romans 12:9). Dishonesty is a failure to love and honor our spouse as we have vowed to do.

Ironically, some people have engaged in dishonesty in an effort to retain a spouse's or family member's love. We say "ironically" because it's not possible to retain love by violating love. A young husband told us how he learned this important lesson: "When my brother and I were growing up, my mother always had dinner on the table for us at 5:30, no matter what else she had to do. My wife is different. Often she hasn't even begun dinner when I get home even though she's been home with the children all day. I used to resent that a lot. But I didn't tell her. I told her it was all right, that I understood, even though I secretly thought she didn't measure up to Mom." He couldn't keep his feelings a secret, however. His wife sensed his disapproval and displeasure and confronted him about it. Each time she did, he denied that he was bothered by the matter. When she insisted that he was certainly bothered about something, he became irritated, and they would begin to argue.

Eventually they worked through the issue, but only after the marriage came perilously close to rupture. Why had he continued to insist, over a period of years, that the issue of meals didn't bother him? "I really love my wife," he told us. "I knew she would be hurt if she realized that I thought she wasn't doing as good a job as my mother did. I didn't want to risk losing her love." As he discovered, the dishonesty posed the greater risk, because it is a violation of love, not a way to retain love.

Part III
The Patterns of Honesty

Instead, speak the truth in love . . .

EPHESIANS 4:15

CHAPTER 8

The Practice of Self-Serving Honesty

When one of the authors (Bob) was the chair of a department in a state university, a professor came in for a chat. The following conversation ensued:

Prof.: "The department seems to be in good shape right now."

Bob: "Yes, I think it is."

Prof.: "Have you had any complaints from students?"

Bob: "About what?"

Prof.: "Anything."

Bob: "Nothing serious. Why?"

Prof.: "I need to tell you that one of my female students may be coming to see you. I was advising her in my office a few days ago and—you know how I am—I was waving my arms around while I talked and brushed against her. She took offense."

Bob: "You need to be careful. But she hasn't come to me yet."

Prof.: "Let me know if she does. I'm sure we can straighten it out."

An honest man? As it turns out, the college dismissed the professor for sexual harassment. His apparently honest admission was an effort first to find out if the student had yet talked to Bob and second to make it appear that he was an innocent victim of a misunderstanding in case she did complain. When he found out that she had not yet formally complained, he went to her and threatened to kick her out of the program if she reported him. She did anyway, and he finally lost his job.

The professor was honest about the incident occurring and about a part of what had happened (brushing against the student). Everything in his conversation was true. It was, however, a good example of what we call "self-serving honesty." Self-serving honesty underscores a point we made at the beginning of this book—that honesty is a complex dynamic. Self-serving honesty comes in a variety of forms.

SUPERFICIAL HONESTY

Once on a flight, a man sitting next to us struck up a conversation. By the time we reached our destination, we knew the man's life history. We heard about his marriage, his divorce, his children, his occupational achievements and frustrations, his vacation in the Bermudas the past summer, and his plans for retirement at age fifty-five. He, on the other hand, knew nothing about us. He didn't even know our names. He asked us nothing about ourselves and told us volumes about himself.

From time to time you will meet people who will share virtually their entire life history the first time you meet. This may seem to create a kind of instant intimacy. Actually, it's at best a pseudo-intimacy, because that person may know little or nothing about you. The person seems to be open and honest, yet it's only a superficial honesty, reflecting the person's need to talk rather than the effort to create intimacy.

Superficial honesty occurs in marriage also. Helen and Rob are a young, two-career couple; Helen is a graphics designer and Rob is a salesperson. Helen, to some extent, and Rob, to a great extent, never seem to run out of words. Even the counselor has to interrupt them at times to be heard. Rob, however, feels that their talkativeness is a positive factor for marriage: "I come from a very verbal family. I admit it. I love to talk. I *need* to talk. I would like to sit up with Helen every night until midnight and just discuss things together. I don't hold anything back. I tell her everything."

At that point, Helen interrupted: "You may think that you like to *discuss* things, but we really don't discuss. I listen, and you talk. I—"

Rob interrupted her: "I want you to talk. Why don't you tell me when you feel I'm not listening to you? I need you to talk to me just as I need to talk to you. I don't want—"

After Helen and Rob interrupted each other a few more times, the counselor broke into their conversation. "I want you to notice the pattern of communication here today. I seem to be the only one who has done much listening. You two both seem to have a problem hearing the other one out. We have a lot of work to do in learning to listen."

Helen and Rob have what appears to be an open, honest marriage, with a good deal of sharing. But their honesty is superficial. Each is fulfilling personal needs for talking, but neither is listening that much to the other. As a result, they have not built an intimate relationship. In fact, as Helen admits, they seem to know little more about each other now than they did when they got married: "I don't always understand Rob. And I don't feel he understands me. They say that communication is the heart of any marriage. But it doesn't seem to help us. No matter how much we talk, we don't seem to get any closer."

Helen and Rob have begun a program of learning how to listen, a topic we will discuss in chapter 11. They need to learn that it doesn't help simply to throw bushels of words at each other. Without listening, they do not have honest sharing.

Honesty can be superficial in a second way, namely, by

using a barrage of words to hide the fact that some of your deepest thoughts and feelings are never expressed. That is, some people share a good deal about themselves, but what they say is fairly superficial.

Don't misunderstand. A certain amount of small talk is important to marital intimacy. Family therapists have found that small talk is a way to communicate interest and acceptance to one's spouse. Yet at some point the sharing has to reach deeper levels. You can't build intimacy by talking only about the weather or the state of the backyard or the color of the neighbor's new car.

One way to get a sense of how balanced your conversations are is to keep a daily record for a few weeks of the topics that you discuss. It's important to note not only the topic but also whether the conversation was just a sharing of facts or included some personal references.

For example, we usually think of talking about the weather as small talk. But a discussion of the weather could involve more. Compare the following three sets of conversations:

She: "It looks as if it's going to rain."

He: "Yes."

She: "You better take an umbrella."

He: "Okay."

She: "It looks as if it's going to rain."

He: "Oh, dear. I better hurry. I don't want to be late for work."

She: "Don't forget to take an umbrella with you."

He: "Right. Thanks for the reminder."

She: "It looks as if it's going to rain.

He: "Oh, dear. I better hurry. I don't want to be late for work, although I'd just as soon stay home today. Rain depresses me."

She: "Don't forget to take an umbrella. We really need this rain. Why do you find it depressing?"

Note the difference in the three conversations. The first is truly small talk—an observation about the weather and a reminder to be prepared for it. The second adds a dimension, the expression of worry about the consequences of the weather and an expression of gratitude about a spouse's thoughtfulness. The third conversation goes even deeper, as the man expresses some general feelings about rainy weather and the woman picks up on his words and pursues the idea with him.

In your record of your conversations, therefore, make a chart with five columns. In the column to the far left, briefly describe the topic of your conversation. Make the next three columns check-mark size and label them *small talk, elaboration*, and *feelings*. The three are represented by the example above.

Don't worry about exact definitions. If you feel the conversation was nothing more than small talk, check that column. Your spouse may or may not agree with you; you may want to discuss your different observations. If you feel, on the other hand, that your conversation went beyond small talk to concentrate on ideas or concerns or feelings about the matter, check one of those columns.

In the fifth column, leave room for comments. For example, note whether any feelings expressed were negative or positive or note what you learned about your spouse from the conversation. In other words, instead of a simple record, you can keep a diary of your conversations over the period of a few weeks and then use it to talk about communication in your marriage.

From the record/diary, you should have a sense of the extent to which your marriage is characterized by superficial honesty. If either you or your spouse rate a major proportion of your conversations as small talk, you need to spend some time with the suggestions in chapter 11 and enhance the quality of your communication.

SELECTIVE HONESTY

Selective honesty is choosing the areas or the times in which you will be honest. It is being honest when it's to your advantage and less than honest when that is to your advantage. This sounds devilishly self-serving, and it can be. Surely, you may think, no Christian would engage in such behavior. Keep in mind, however, that it is easy to justify dishonest behavior and think of it not as dishonesty but as a sincere effort to maintain a strong marriage. Also keep in mind that we are not always aware of our dishonesty. Sometimes we just react to something without thinking about what we are doing. Only on reflection is it clear that the reaction was a dishonest one.

For example, a young, second-generation Asian-American couple was having serious disagreements about a variety of areas of married life. After listening to their two points of view for a while, the counselor raised the question, "How rooted are you in Korean culture?" The couple looked puzzled for a moment, then the counselor explained to the husband, "I'm finding it difficult to understand your reactions to your wife. Sometimes it seems to me that you respond to her as an American would. At other times, it seems that you act more as I would expect a Korean to act."

The husband reflected on the counselor's observations, then laughed, and said somewhat shamefacedly, "I guess you're right. I guess I use whichever one is more useful to me at the time. Sometimes I treat her as if we're both Americans, and sometimes—especially when I want her just to follow my wishes and not question me—I treat her the way my father treated my mother."

His wife's eyes grew wide as he spoke. "That's true," she agreed. "That's why I told you that you seem like two different people to me." This insight didn't immediately solve all their problems, but it gave both the husband and wife an understanding they hadn't had before. He was not aware of the extent to which he had switched back and forth between American and Korean patterns to serve his own purposes.

We are all tempted to selective honesty. Recall that Paul had to confront Peter over the issue of eating with Gentiles: "Before certain men came from James, he used to eat with the Gentiles. But when they arrived, he began to draw back and separate himself from the Gentiles because he was afraid of those who belonged to the circumcision group. The other Jews joined him in his hypocrisy, so that by their hypocrisy even Barnabas was led astray" (Gal. 2:12–13).

In Peter's case, it was fear of the Jews' disapproval that led him to be dishonest about his relationship to Gentile Christians. Fear is a common reason for selective dishonesty in marriage. People fear that their spouses will think less of them or will get angry with them or will not love them anymore. Rather than risk an unpleasant or painful situation, they choose dishonesty.

Terri, a thirty-seven-year-old teacher, came to counseling after reading women's magazines that talked about a woman's need for, and right to, sexual fulfillment. Terri told the counselor that she had never found sex fulfilling in the seven years of her marriage. The counselor had Terri bring her husband to the next session so that they could work together on the problem. At first Terri refused. She just wanted to work on it by herself, she said. But when the counselor persisted, Terri told him that her husband had no idea she felt the way she did. "I always wanted him to be happy with me, and I heard about men who had affairs because their wives weren't sexually satisfying to them. So I've pretended to have orgasms, but I don't think I actually have ever had one."

With the help of the counselor, Terri told her husband about the problem and got him to agree to come with her. Her husband was startled when she first told him. Fortunately, he was understanding and eager to find a solution to the problem. He was also somewhat dismayed that Terri had been dishonest with him about their sexual relationship; in every other area, they had an honest marriage. Yet in their love making, as Terri said, "I was just afraid of what would happen if I told him. So I faked it."

Terri knew what she was doing. In other cases, as we have pointed out, people are unaware of being selectively dishonest. You can examine your own marriage and search for selective dishonesty by thinking about how you relate to your spouse in each of the following areas:

- communication
- disagreements and conflict
- parenting
- spiritual matters
- friends
- members of your extended families
- income and expenses
- affection and sex
- leisure activities
- your spouse's behavior, including any annoying habits

You can't go through the above list quickly. You need to spend time with each area. It might be best to do one area a day until you are through the list. Think carefully about all your interaction with your spouse in that area and pray for help to be candid with yourself about whether you are honest with your spouse.

TRANSPARENT HONESTY

As we noted in chapter 1, some marriage experts have said that spouses must be totally transparent with each other, revealing everything that they think or feel. We need to look a little more closely at this kind of honesty, because some Christians think that transparent honesty is in accord with the teachings of Jesus. But as we will show in subsequent chapters, transparent honesty is not the Christian way for a marriage.

Jesus himself did not practice it. Think, for instance,

of the cryptic answers he sometimes gave to questions. When the disciples asked why he spoke to the people in parables, he replied, "The knowledge of the secrets of the kingdom of heaven has been given to you, but not to them. Whoever has will be given more, and he will have an abundance. Whoever does not have, even what he has will be taken from him. This is why I speak to them in parables: 'Though seeing, they do not see; though hearing, they do not hear or understand'" (Matt. 13:11–13).

Whether the answer was clear to the disciples, we do not know. Certainly, its meaning to the rest of us has been debated for centuries.

Transparent honesty, then, is not the Christian way. On the contrary, transparent honesty is self-serving. Let us explain at least two ways in which transparent honesty is oriented toward our own needs rather than other's needs. First, we have seen people use transparent honesty to assuage their sense of guilt and to do so by confessing their sins indiscriminately. Recall the story of Dan and Sharon in chapter 1. Clearly, Dan was serving his own needs in being honest with Sharon about his attraction to his student. He needed to confess to someone because he felt guilty. It would have been better, however, if Dan had confessed it to someone other than Sharon.

Confession is important and necessary, of course, but people should not confess indiscriminately or thoughtlessly to other people. Sharon certainly feels that Dan's confession was for his needs, not hers. "Some of my Christian friends tell me that I had a right to know. I remind them that after he told me, Dan felt fine, but I was totally miserable. Dan was only taking care of his own guilt. He wasn't helping me one bit."

Sharon's point is a good one. Before being transparently honest about something that makes you feel guilty and that could hurt your spouse, you should ask a number of questions:

- How will my spouse benefit? How will my spouse feel?
- How will our relationship benefit?
- Am I doing this to help my spouse and our relationship, or am I mainly concerned with relieving my own guilt?
- If I need to talk about the matter, to whom should I talk?
- If I need to confess, to whom should I confess?

If the matter is something that could potentially hurt your spouse, you should probably talk to a pastor or counselor and explore the above questions.

The second way in which transparent honesty is self-serving is when it is used to avoid change. Some people openly acknowledge some kind of sin or shortcoming only to continue behaving in the same way! In effect, they are saying: This is the way I am, so I must continue to behave as I have been doing. Transparent honesty thereby relieves them (at least in their own thinking) of the need for changing their behavior.

This kind of self-serving honesty may be seen in:

- the husband who always forgets his anniversary because "I never have been any good at remembering dates";
- the wife who is always late because "I've always had a hard time getting ready to go anywhere";
- the husband who flirts with other women, even in the presence of his wife because "I have a strong sex drive, and I really find nearly all women attractive";
- the wife who regularly overdraws a checking account because "I'm not good with numbers";
- the husband who spends countless hours watching sporting events on television because "I've always been a sports nut."

All of these comments involve what logicians call a *non sequitur*. That is, it may be true that a man has never been good at remembering dates, but it does not follow that he must necessarily forget his anniversary. Or it may be true that a woman has never been good with numbers, but it does not necessarily follow that she must overdraw her checking account with some regularity. To say "that is the way I am" is not to say "that is the way I have to be."

We'll illustrate the point with the story of Tommy and Cindy. Their marriage was marred by one recurring problem: Tommy frequently made remarks that Cindy viewed as hurtful because they suggested to her that he disapproved of her behavior. Cindy explained the problem to us. "Tommy has very high standards, and I appreciate that about him. But sometimes it really hurts when he makes me feel as if I never measure up to his standards. Like cleaning the house. He works on Saturday mornings, so that's when I clean the house. Last Saturday he came home, and what's the first thing he says after I've worked hard all morning? He says that I didn't get the kitchen sink completely clean! And he does that kind of thing to me all the time. Not just about housecleaning, but about a lot of other things as well."

Tommy agreed that he had high standards and was demanding. The problems in their marriage could be solved quickly, he said, if Cindy just realized and accepted what kind of person he was. "I'm just a blunt guy. I say what I think. I'm not trying to hurt her. I'm just telling her the way I see it. Why should she be hurt by that? If I don't measure up at work, I get told about it. And I want that. It helps me do a better job. That's all I'm trying to do for Cindy."

At first Tommy failed to see two important things about his bluntness: it was hurting Cindy, and, contrary to what he implied, he wasn't stuck with being blunt. Once he acknowledged how much he was hurting Cindy, Tommy learned to behave differently. For example, instead of coming home and pointing out what she had not done properly, he learned to compliment her on what she had done well. He also expressed appreciation for the fact that she did the housework even though she worked outside the home nearly as many hours a week as he did.

Tommy learned to modify his bluntness in other situations as well. He used to hurt Cindy by criticizing her choice of dress. If he didn't like a particular dress, he simply would say something like, "You look lousy in that thing." Now they have agreed that he will do one of two things: either he will go with her and help her pick out clothing that they both agree looks attractive on her, or he will say nothing about her choices unless she asks.

As Tommy learned, whenever we are transparently honest in order to avoid change, we fall short of our calling. By saying, "I'm just a blunt guy," Tommy was neither sorry nor honest in a Christian sense. He was simply self-serving, trying to justify an unChristian form of behavior that he didn't want to change.

As Tommy and Cindy's story illustrates, transparent honesty is not only self-serving but also hurtful to others. Because many regard it as the Christian ideal, we will look at some of the dangers of this self-serving behavior more closely in the next chapter.

CHAPTER 9

The Dangers of Transparent Honesty

Jacob, or Israel, had twelve sons. He was transparently honest about the way he felt about his youngest, Joseph: "Now Israel loved Joseph more than any of his other sons, because he had been born to him in his old age; and he made a richly ornamented robe for him. When his brothers saw that their father loved him more than any of them, they hated him and could not speak a kind word to him" (Gen. 37:3–4).

This story underscores two important points about transparent honesty. First, such honesty is expressed in deeds as well as words. Recall the story of Cindy and Tommy in the last chapter. At times, Tommy would convey his displeasure without saying a word—a look of disgust, a shake of the head, or a loud sigh.

Second, transparent honesty is more likely to harm than to help your marriage and your family life. We have seen one important reason for the damage that transparent honesty brings to relationships; namely, it tends to be self-serving. Anything that is self-serving is not likely to enhance the quality of an intimate relationship.

Let's look at a number of other reasons why transparent honesty is damaging to intimate relationships. As we discuss them, you will see that transparent honesty is as dangerous for a healthy marriage as is dishonesty.

TRANSPARENT HONESTY HURTS

One of the ironies of transparent honesty is that most people who practice it consider it to be both Christian and helpful. However, the opposite is true: transparent honesty hurts others and hurts the relationship. The hurt can come about through honest deeds, honest words, or both. Furthermore, it can involve an isolated incident, or it can be a more systematic kind of hurting.

Incidents that Hurt

At one time or another, probably most people will hurt a spouse in an incident involving transparent honesty. To an outsider, the incident may appear to be relatively trivial. Yet to the people involved, it can be significant and quite painful.

Brad, a civil engineer who has been married for twelve years, told us about an "awful thing" he had done to his wife some years earlier. Brad and his wife had been arguing about something. "I don't even remember now what it was about," he said. However, he recalls being very angry with his wife. And before they had settled the argument, they had to go to his parents' house for dinner. Both maintained an icy silence all the way to dinner. Clearly, they still felt very angry.

At Brad's parents' house, the dinner proceeded smoothly, with the usual family talk and with Brad and his wife giving no indication that they had been arguing. After dinner, Brad's wife and mother did the dishes, while Brad and his father sat in the living room chatting. Soon, his father dozed off. Shortly after that, Brad's wife came into the room, the dish towel draped over her arm. "She asked me if I would like another cup of coffee. She had a slight smile on her face. I knew what that meant. She wanted our disagreement to end. She wanted to make peace. But I was still angry, and I wanted her to know I was angry. I remember thinking to myself that I wasn't going to keep pretending that everything was fine, even if my parents did find out, So I didn't say anything to her. I just looked at her and made a face then picked up a magazine and pretended to read."

Brad looked pained as he continued. He told us he could see the tears come into his wife's eyes. Then she hurried back into the kitchen. He just sat there. The momentary feeling of triumph that he had experienced because of his "honest" revelation of his feelings quickly faded into a sense of misery. He still remembers the incident as one of the meaner things he ever did to his wife. He also has some interesting comments to make about transparent honesty as a result of the experience. "It happened about eight years ago. The only good thing I can say about the event is that it taught me how horribly selfish it is for me to abuse my wife—or other people, for that matter—by insisting that she always has to know exactly how I feel. I can tell you that I've been careful ever since. I have a wonderful Christian wife and a wonderful Christian home, and I'm determined not to let anything ruin it, especially not my own petty feelings."

Systematic Hurting

Systematic hurting is hurting as an ongoing, regular kind of activity. The hurting may occur through regular deeds; if, for example, Brad had continued to show his anger or frustration or displeasure by gestures or other behavior, he would be involved in systematic hurting by deeds.

The hurting may also occur through words. Let's look at the example of Chris and Allison. We first became acquainted with them at a community function. We found that we had a lot in common. We had children about the same age, belonged to the same denomination, and had

many of the same interests. We began doing things together. Shortly after we met, we made plans to go out to
dinner and a movie.

It was that first dinner that gave us a new perspective
of Chris and Allison and their marriage. We were discussing
the declining SAT scores in public schools. Allison said that
in her opinion the quality of teaching was as much to blame
as anything else. Chris laughed and quickly jumped in with,
"As usual, you're criticizing something you know nothing
about. The teaching is as good as it ever was."

Allison blushed slightly, and said, "Oh, I know I don't
really know much about it. But I just meant that I had heard
from some of the kids in the neighborhood that their
teachers weren't always very good in the classroom."

This was the first of an ongoing series of put-downs we
heard from Chris. Allison always seemed to take them in
stride, laughing them off or ignoring them or treating them
as if they were a form of teasing. Once, for instance, Chris
remarked that Allison should not express political views
before checking with him, since she just gave opinions off
the top of her head. She slapped his arm lightly and said,
"You just act as if women have no sense. Wait until you have
to deal with a woman president." Chris just groaned, and
the conversation took a different turn.

Over a period of months, we observed a number of
things about Chris and Allison. First, the verbal put-downs
were fairly regular. Second, Chris was aware that we did not
find his remarks humorous even though he usually preced-
ed them with a laugh. Third, Chris frequently tried, by both
verbal and nonverbal means, to make it appear that his
remarks were mostly teasing.

After some months, Allison admitted that his remarks
hurt her. She only pretended to laugh them off because she
didn't want to embarrass him or start an argument in
public. However, she had confronted Chris about his verbal
abuse in private many times. "I've told him how hurtful his
words are and how inadequate they make me feel," she said.
"My hurt and damaged self-esteem have not stopped him,

however. Over the years I have come to the conclusion that Chris really is abusive. His continual put-downs hurt just as much as if he physically struck me."

Chris and Allison eventually separated. The separation lasted for a couple of years. Only after Chris agreed to get counseling did Allison agree to return to him. For our purposes here, it's important to note one thing: in talking with Chris one day, we found out that his remarks, while sometimes overstating the case, actually did reflect his feelings about Allison: "You have to understand that I really love Allison. But she doesn't know beans about the stuff she's always spouting off about. She talks without thinking. I might exaggerate sometimes, but I'm only telling the truth. I'm sorry it hurts her, but don't you think she needs to hear the truth?"

We pointed out that he was really talking about the "truth" as he saw it, not necessarily the truth as others might see it. We didn't find Allison to be the "cute but vacant-headed creature" Chris thought he had married. She didn't have as much education as Chris had, but she was quite thoughtful and had some excellent insights about what was going on in the world. At times, she did make some comments that were "off-the-wall," but they were less common than her more thoughtful statements.

Even if what Chris had said was wholly accurate, however, his half-teasing, half-serious way of continually pointing it out to Allison was unnecessarily hurtful to her. Allison told us that she knew that sometimes she made "dumb statements." She didn't need Chris to reinforce the point and to make her feel as if it applied to most of what she said.

Chris's attempt to tell his wife what he honestly thought of her nearly cost him his marriage. He is doing much better now. He still criticizes some of the things she says, but he also praises some of her insights. Chris and Allison are going to make it.

MANY THOUGHTS AND FEELINGS ARE TRANSITORY

Another reason that transparent honesty is dangerous is that we all have transitory thoughts and feelings that could damage our intimate relationships. We don't act on them. And they don't even represent the way we feel generally. To share them with our spouse, therefore, could both give a false impression of how we really feel and also hurt the relationship. The actual impact, however, depends on whether the transitory thoughts and feelings are negative or positive. Let's look at the negative ones first.

Expressing Transitory, Negative Thoughts and Feelings

Not all people blurt out whatever they are thinking or feeling at the moment. For example, Bill is a salesperson who faces many pressures at work. He told us that he knows he sometimes gets angrier at his wife than she deserves. "I'm just frustrated because of my work, and unfortunately I take my frustrations out on her. When that happens, the thought may come into my mind that it would be nice to be single again. That would be one less problem in my life."

Bill went on to say, however, that he never expresses that thought to his wife. "I love being married. I know I don't really want to be without her. And I know it would hurt Janet if I said that I wished I were single again. So I just bite my tongue on that one, and soon the feeling passes."

Bill's fantasy about being single again probably occurs at some time or other with most people. Bill has good judgment in not expressing such thoughts to his wife. Not everyone is as sensible nor as sensitive.

Here are some examples of the kinds of transitory thoughts and feelings that you may experience, along with the sort of things that you might say if you were being transparently honest with your spouse:

- You intensely dislike your spouse for saying or doing something that embarrasses you; you say: "I hate you. You made a fool of yourself in front of my friends."

- You are at a party, and you meet someone whom you find sexually attractive; you say: "Did you see that person I just met? What a sexy creature! My heart is about to jump out of my chest. I haven't felt like this in years."
- Your spouse is inept at something, and you feel as if he or she is temporarily without sense; you say: "For crying out loud, it's simple. I don't think you have the brains of a two-year-old."
- Your spouse looks particularly haggard one morning, and you wonder if you will continue to find him or her romantic; you say: "Boy, you look as if you really feel rotten this morning. I feel as if I'm married to an old woman [or man]."
- You've had a stressful day working, your spouse seems not to understand how you feel, and you think you are married to an uncaring and insensitive clod; you say: "I detest the way you sit there and think only about yourself. Why don't you ever care about my feelings?"

Admittedly, some of these responses represent situations in which something *should* be said. It should be obvious, however, that the kind of blunt sharing of thoughts and feelings in these examples would do little for the quality of any relationship. We can find effective ways to express how we think and feel and to raise our concerns without giving our spouse the impression that our momentary state represents the way we generally feel.

But aren't the above examples exaggerated? Would anyone actually say such things? The answer in both cases is yes. Transparent honesty, however, need not be as crass as the examples we described in order to damage a relationship.

Jodi and Darren have been married seven years. The marriage is beginning to look more solid after a number of years of deterioration. The problem is Darren's temper. Usually, Darren is outgoing, genial, interesting, and good-natured.

During the courtship years, Jodi saw Darren get very angry with others, but he never blew up at her. Besides, his anger peaked quickly and went away quickly. He never held a grudge against anyone. After they were married, the pressures of carving out a career, earning a living, and paying for a house overwhelmed Darren at times, and he would explode in anger over something Jodi did or said.

As always, the anger subsided quickly. And Jodi knew that his anger came from the stress and frustration he felt at work. She could handle that. What she couldn't handle were his remarks. "When Darren gets angry, he says things that really hurt me. Like the other day. I could tell when he got home that he was feeling stressed. So I decided to try to take his mind off the work and help him relax. I suggested we go out for dinner and then take a walk in the park nearby. He always enjoys that.

"But this time he got terribly irritable and told me that we couldn't afford to eat out so much, that I needed to be more responsible about meals, that I wasn't carrying my share of the burden."

Darren's remarks were not as blunt as some of the examples we gave earlier. Nevertheless, they cut deeply. And they hurt even though Jodi knew that he didn't generally feel that way. "I know that Darren doesn't *really* think I'm irresponsible. I know he appreciates all that I do. And I know that he really loves me. But when he says those things, it tears me apart. I'm ready to leave him on the spot."

Darren articulated only his transitory feelings and thoughts when he was angry. Learning to control his anger, which meant learning to control what he said when he was angry, brought new life into his marriage.

In summary, to have an honest marriage does *not* mean that we share every passing thought or feeling with our spouses. We need to be transparent with God. We must not be transparent with our spouses, at least not with those transitory, negative thoughts and feelings that we all experience.

Expressing Transitory, Positive Thoughts and Feelings

However, not all transitory thoughts and feelings are damaging to a relationship. Some should be shared, even though they don't represent the way you generally feel. We recommend that couples learn to express their transitory, positive thoughts and feelings. When they are shared, they enrich the marriage. When they remain private, they become another part of the store of secrets that depress the quality of the marriage.

We say "learn to express" them because we live in a culture that teaches us in many ways to articulate negative but not positive comments about others. For example, studies of interaction between mothers and their children in a play setting find that the bulk of the mothers' talk involves such things as correcting, guiding, and cautioning. Only a very small part involves praise and other positive comments.

Or think about when you were in school. Whatever you did wrong, your teachers were sure to point out. How often did a teacher praise you for making a good point or doing good work? We once heard a college professor say that he had trained himself to spot mistakes quickly in students' work. He prided himself on being able to go through written work quickly and mark all the errors. To our knowledge, he never wrote comments of praise on students' papers.

The outcome of growing up in such a society is that we all learn to identify and remark on the mistakes, the shortcomings, the negative aspects of others. If we are silent about anything, it is likely to be the positive things.

The point is that we generally tend to admire in silence and criticize openly, and we are even more likely to do so with transitory feelings and thoughts. We urge you, therefore, to articulate them when they are positive and appropriate.

For example, suppose you experience a sudden flush of loving feeling for your spouse. Sometimes it can almost take you by surprise. As one wife told us, "We were just sitting at breakfast, each of us reading the paper. I looked at him, and suddenly I felt this overwhelming sense of love. I wanted to go over to him and hug him and tell him how much he means to me."

Did she? No.

Why not? "I'm not sure. I guess it seemed like a foolish thing to do. I mean, if he asked me, I couldn't even tell him why I suddenly felt that way. I went back to my paper, and the feeling subsided. But I really enjoyed it for the moment."

Unfortunately, she deprived her husband of a special moment. Such feelings should be shared. She could have simply said: "You know, I don't understand why I suddenly feel this way, but at this moment I love you more than I ever have before." No one would have thought that foolish. Her husband probably would have been thrilled.

A husband acknowledged the same problem when he admitted that he had given his wife "untold numbers" of "secret compliments." He explained what he meant: "Sometimes I see her when she's dressed and ready for work, and I think to myself, *Wow, she sure looks great today.* But I don't tell her that. Or she speaks to our church group, and I think to myself, *Wow, she sure is an effective servant of the Lord.* But I usually don't say anything to her about it."

This particular husband is working on his problem. He grew up in a family in which no one complimented anyone else. It's hard for him to articulate some of the thoughts and feelings he has. For years, therefore, he was a secret admirer of his own wife! Now he is working on becoming an open admirer.

Let's take this a step further. We recommend not only that you articulate such thoughts and feelings to your spouse but that you actively work on *creating* as well as expressing them. Try this exercise. Each week, observe your spouse carefully and try to find something that you admire or appreciate. You will probably discover that you admire and appreciate a lot that you have tended to take for granted. You will also probably find yourself experiencing a good deal more positive, transitory thoughts and feelings. Share those with your spouse and see what happens to the quality of your relationship. Among other things, you probably will find that your spouse will start expressing more positive things too.

TRANSPARENT HONESTY CAN MASK PROBLEMS

The third way in which transparent honesty is dangerous is that it can mask rather than illuminate problems in a marriage. Supposedly, one of the benefits of transparent honesty is that it eliminates the problems that arise from secret thoughts and feelings. Ironically, the transparently honest person is more likely to obscure problems. In other words, transparent honesty can really be a form of dishonesty, because the real problem remains hidden.

Recall the situation of Bill and Janet we discussed earlier. If Bill had told Janet that he wished he had not married, it would have made her think their relationship was in serious trouble. However, Bill's problem was really his work. The pressures of his job made him frustrated and anxious. The single life symbolized a less stressful and more carefree time in his life. Fortunately, Bill was wise enough to realize that the relationship he needed to change was the one at work and not at home.

Yet think of the damage that could have been done if Bill had expressed his feelings at the moment. His words could have seriously hurt Janet. Worse yet, if he had acted on them, he could have ended his marriage only to find that being single was not the solution to his problems. Farfetched? Not really. We have known several people who have blamed their marriage for their personal unhappiness only to find that after they ended the relationship, their unhappiness was still with them.

In other words, quite often the way we feel or think about our spouse at the moment is not the root of the problem. When we are emotionally distraught, all of our normal feelings about things and people can become distorted. To express feelings or thoughts about our spouse at such a time, therefore, may only obscure the problem. To act on them will certainly compound our difficulties.

The Triple Low

According to the theory of biorhythms, we all have three monthly cycles. Over the course of each month, our emotional, intellectual, and physical functioning all vary, each having both a high and a low point. They don't vary according to quite the same schedule, however. You could, on a given day for instance, be at an intellectual high, a physical low, and an emotional midpoint. Sometime (not every month) you are at a triple high, other times you're at a triple low. According to the theory, when you are at a triple low, you need to be cautious because you will be prone to mistakes, accidents, and other kinds of malfunctioning.

Now we don't believe that it's possible to predict just when you are at a triple low, but we do believe that each of us has the three cycles. We've all experienced days when we were emotionally high, and it was good to be alive; days when we felt physically capable of doing anything; or times when we felt particularly sharp intellectually. We also all have experienced days when our emotions seemed particularly fragile for no apparent reason or when we felt physically below par or when our minds and tongues seemed to be on vacation.

On those triple-low days, you need to be careful about your feelings for your spouse. Imagine the following conversation taking place when this husband is at a triple low and is also a person who believes in transparent honesty:

She: "You look glum today. What's wrong?"

He: "I don't know. I just feel really low."

144

She: "Well surely you have some idea of why you feel that way."

He: "Not a clue."

She: "Is something bothering you?"

He: "Well, right now *you're* bothering me with all your dumb questions."

She: "So you're mad at me about something."

He: "I didn't say I was mad at you."

She: "What have I done?"

We have moved from the normal below-par feelings on a triple-low day to an expression of concern to a full-fledged argument. What began as a normal human response ended up in an interpersonal conflict.

More than one couple has followed a similar sequence. One spouse blurts out his or her momentary feelings, and the other is offended. It becomes very difficult under such circumstances to deal in a helpful way with the problem because the couple's attention is deflected from the real problem.

Displaced Aggression

Taking your anger out on someone or something other than the cause of the anger is common. Psychologists call it displaced aggression.

A news article some years ago told about a New York man who had an argument with his wife, walked out of his apartment, and in the heat of his anger hit the first man he met in the nose. The man he hit turned out to be a detective. The angry man paid dearly for his displaced aggression.

Displaced anger happens for a number of reasons. It may be that the source of the anger is something that can't be attacked directly, like a stock market that falls when you need it to rise. It may be that the source of the anger is something valuable but frustrating, like a new computer that doesn't seem to work properly for you. It may be that the source of the anger is someone you can't confront directly, such as a boss who would fire you if you complained about being mistreated.

For whatever reasons, the man in the news story felt that he could not directly confront his wife with his anger. In many cases, however, the reverse occurs: the source of the anger is somewhere else, and the spouse becomes the victim.

Nancy and Jim have a good marriage overall. Both struggle as they try to balance the demands of careers with the need to nurture their relationship and the need to grow as Christians by serving the Lord.

In other words, Nancy and Jim typically have a lot of pressure. In the middle of a heated argument one evening, Nancy told Jim that she "hated him." Jim was devastated and was afraid that their relationship was disintegrating. It took several weeks for Nancy to reassure him that she still loved him and that her hateful words had nothing to do with him. Nancy's outburst had resulted from a series of stressful events that caused her to explode that day in rage against everything and everyone in her life. At that moment she "hated" not only her husband but also her mother, her best friend, her boss, and the paper carrier, because they were a part of the general situation that was causing her so much stress.

Again, an honest sharing of a momentary feeling caused much grief. As Nancy recalls the incident, "About an hour later, I could have bitten my tongue off. I cried that night because I could see how hurt Jim was. He's always been a little insecure about our relationship. That night he dreamt that I left him."

Nancy says she has learned one very important thing from that incident: she will not argue with Jim again while her emotions are so intense that she can't control what she says. It's a good rule to follow. We'll return to it in chapter 12, when we talk about the appropriate way for a Christian couple to handle conflict.

Displaced Boredom

You won't find the term "displaced boredom" in psychology books. We coined it to describe a phenomenon that we sometimes observe in marriages. When people who divorce are asked why they have divorced, a substantial number mention, among other things, being bored with the relationship. We believe that in most cases it is a displaced boredom.

Displaced boredom occurs in two ways. First, a person may be bored with work and with the nature of his or her life generally and displace that boredom onto the marital relationship. This is similar to what we discussed above with displaced aggression.

When bored with life generally, a person is vulnerable to the temptation to think that the spouse is the source of the problem. Then statements such as the following can occur:

- "You're no fun anymore."
- "All the excitement is gone from our relationship."
- "I just don't feel any passion for you anymore."

Translated into reality, the three statements are really saying,

- "I get no pleasure out of life right now."
- "Everything in my life is stale to me."
- "I don't have any strong feelings about anything."

When the statements are phrased in terms of the relationship, attention tends to be diverted from the real problem. When they are phrased in the way we translated them, they open up the possibility of discussing the real problem. The point is, both sets of statements reflect the way the speaker feels at the moment. But the second set is more accurate and certainly more helpful.

The second way in which displaced boredom occurs is when it *is* the marriage, and not life generally, that has become boring. We have known a number of couples, particularly several who were married for more than ten years, who acknowledge that they are bored with their marital relationship. Everything from household tasks to leisure activities to sex has become routine. The whole marriage is emotionally flat.

When people are bored with their marriage, they may make statements similar to those suggested earlier. In this case, the boredom is still displaced, because the person is, in essence, saying to the spouse "you are the problem" rather than "we have a problem." However, a boring relationship is never the problem of only one of the spouses.

In other words, if you are bored with your marriage, then you as well as your spouse must assume responsibility for changing the relationship. Boredom occurs, and it occurs among large numbers of couples. Yet it is neither necessary nor inevitable. And if it does creep in, then you both must take responsibility for getting rid of it.

Some therapists and marriage-enrichment leaders talk about "reromanticizing" your marriage. It's a practice that needs to be done with regularity in order to avoid boredom. It can also pull you out of boredom. And it is relatively easy for any couple to practice.

Here is one example of a reromanticizing exercise (all of them require you and your spouse to work together). Take a sheet of paper and write a list of what you would regard as the most romantic times in all the years you have known each other. Write at the top: "I felt really loved by you when . . ." Complete as many answers as you can. Some of the answers may sound silly or may involve things you would no longer want your spouse to do. For instance, you could write: "You rubbed your finger down my nose and then kissed it." Even if that would no longer thrill you, write it down. It helps to remember the magical moments in your past; such memories can warm you and recapture some of the lost romance.

When you have completed your answers, write down a second phrase: "I felt that I was expressing my love for you when . . ." Again, complete as many answers as you can. Then exchange papers and go over each other's list. Discuss your answers. Decide which of the gestures or events would still be romantic for you. Talk about what other kinds of things you might do to regenerate the feelings of romance. Then draw up a plan that will guide each of you to do or say certain things on a regular basis.

Your plan may be more or less specific. For example, we have known some couples who commit themselves to do something special for each other at least once a week. They don't say, and don't even know, in advance what they will do. But they are committed to a weekly, romanticizing surprise. Others will be more specific. For instance, you might agree to take over a chore that your spouse dislikes or give each other a "love you" call on the telephone each day or find a small gift to give to each other each month.

It will take some time and effort, but the only thing you have to lose is boredom.

CHAPTER 10

The Practice
of Loving Honesty

*T*hey were each only thirty years old, but they had been through a lot together. The young couple sat with the minister in a premarital counseling session, and she told about her five-year battle with drugs. During those years her fiancé had helped get her into a rehabilitation program and had supported her in her efforts to "get clean." She had been drug-free for two years when they decided to get married.

"Tell me something that you like best about each other," said the minister.

The young woman spoke first. She didn't need any time to think about her answer. "I love his honesty. I know that when I go to him, I'll always get an honest response. I may not always like it at first. But it's really important to me. It's one of the things that's helped me get off drugs."

The young woman touched on one of the values of an honest relationship: it enables us to cope with our problems. We have to be able to trust our spouse to be honest with us if we are to grow, cope with problems, and build an enriching life together. However, the various kinds of selfish honesty that we have discussed will not achieve those aims. An honest marriage needs loving honesty.

Loving honesty takes two forms: monitored honesty and change honesty. And in contrast to the various kinds of selfish honesty, each of these two forms focuses on the relationship rather than on individual needs.

MONITORED HONESTY

One form of loving honesty is what we call *monitored honesty*. It refers to Paul's idea of "speaking the truth in love" and James' point that Christians need to "keep a tight rein" on their tongues (Eph. 4:15; James 1:26). Some Christians feel that monitored honesty is a form of deceit. Let's examine the issue carefully.

The Call to Honesty

We want to be clear at the outset of our discussion: deceit is not a godly attribute. Jesus said that it's not what goes into a person that makes him or her evil, but what comes out—including deceit (Mark 7:17–23). Deceit is a characteristic of the ungodly (Rom. 1:29). The chief priests and elders used deceit to arrest and kill Jesus (Matt. 26:4).

Deceit is pervasive in our lives today. For example, stories of deception abound in the area of government, from the Gulf of Tonkin resolution that justified the expansion of the Vietnam War on the basis of false information to the congresspeople who wrote millions of dollars worth of bad checks. In education, prestigious universities have been faulted for misusing money given for research, spending it on parties and personal items for the researchers. In religion, televangelists have been fined and even sent to prison for violating federal laws. In medicine, doctors have been prosecuted for fraud in Medicare and Medicaid payments, and researchers have been disgraced for fabricating research results. In family life, infidelity mars anywhere from a third to a half of all marriages.

In such a world, Christians must witness to the transforming power of Christ by shunning deceit. In all areas of our lives, including our intimate relationships, the Gospel calls us to be honest.

Jesus set the example for us. There was no deceit to be found in his mouth (1 Peter 2:22). Not everyone liked the responses he gave, but he deceived no one.

We value that kind of honesty. We treasure the person to whom we can go and "get a straight answer." The young woman we discussed at the beginning of this chapter underscored the importance of honesty in marriage when she said, "I know that honesty will be a vital ingredient after we marry, just as it's been during our courtship. If I can't be sure of my husband's honesty with me, I can't be sure of anything in this life."

The sticky problem, then, is not whether honesty is an essential element of a Christian marriage but exactly what we mean by honesty in Christian marriage.

Honesty in Speech

As we have stressed, honesty in speech does not mean transparent honesty. What, then, does it mean to speak honestly with your spouse? In essence, honesty in speech must be guided by the twin principles of speaking the truth in love and keeping a rein on the tongue. While transparent honesty says anything and everything, loving honesty monitors thoughts and feelings.

We must, as James puts it, "keep a tight rein" on our tongues. The phrase suggests a picture of a horse that is kept under control. Without a rein, the horse goes wherever it pleases. People who don't keep a tight rein on their tongues say anything that comes to mind. It doesn't matter if what is said is snide, hurtful, insensitive, or crude. It's as if they have no shutoff valve between the brain and the tongue. Nothing monitors and filters the thoughts.

Some years ago a man with whom we had counseled invited us to attend a dinner hosted by his parents. The man's mother punctuated the night with a series of blunt and crude remarks. To a woman who had come in a sporty outfit, the mother said loudly, "You're dressed like a gypsy. Are you a gypsy?" To a man who declined to eat the meat, explaining with a slight blush that he was a vegetarian, she said, "What's wrong with meat? It doesn't hurt anyone else. Why should it hurt you?" She said similar things to others throughout the evening.

The mother's remarks turned the dinner into an unsettling ordeal. She had been a transparently honest woman all her life. She would certainly assure us that she meant no harm by what she said. Moreover, she probably wasn't even aware of how uncomfortable she made her guests. She had, after all, related this way to her husband for over forty years.

At times we all have insensitive, caustic, or hurtful thoughts. We can't always keep these thoughts from popping into our minds. But James' point is that we don't have to speak them. He argues that we can't say we are religious unless we have learned not to articulate them.

Some Christians feel this is hypocritical. After all, if we have thoughts or feelings about someone, isn't it the Christian thing to be honest and let the person know? Not according to James. A Christian, he urges, has the power to control those thoughts and feelings so they don't hurt and damage others.

Why isn't that deceit? The difference between deceit and monitored honesty lies in the question of who benefits. We use deceit to advance personal causes or selfish interests. We choose monitored honesty to speak the truth in love and at the same time protect others and honor the name of Christ.

Anything Versus Everything

Monitored honesty in marriage means that you can tell your spouse anything, but you are not obligated to tell your spouse everything. That is, if you have a solid, trusting relationship with your spouse, you should be able to share anything—your thoughts, your feelings, your fears, your anxieties, your aspirations, your dreams. At the same time, that doesn't mean that you tell your spouse everything.

If you are about to say something that might upset your spouse, ask yourself a number of questions first.

- Is what I am about to say important to our relationship, or is it just a passing thought or feeling?
- Will what I am about to say hurt my spouse or damage our relationship?
- Is what I am about to say something that my spouse can correct or change?

For example, it may be true that you don't like your mother-in-law. If your spouse understands the basis for your attitude, you can probably discuss your feelings with him or her. As one husband put it, "My mother-in-law is domineering and controlling. I just avoid her as much as possible. My wife knows how her mother is and understands my behavior. We openly discuss the situation, and this has helped my wife as well as me deal with the problem."

But other cases of in-law problems are more complex. Kay has been married to Greg for eighteen years. They have a strong marriage, but Kay doesn't like her father-in-law, who is self-centered and extremely critical and demanding of his family. Kay resents the way he uses feelings of guilt to manipulate them.

"No matter what Greg does," she told us, "it's never enough." Kay particularly resents the way that Greg's father expects them to make him their first priority. "We visit him every week. But if we have a holiday, he expects us to come twice that week. Once on a holiday, he called and asked Greg what we were doing. Greg told him we were both tired and just wanted to relax. He said that was good—we could come over and relax with him.

"Worse than that was last year when we went on

vacation. He got mad at us for leaving town. Greg called him every couple of days. And when we got back, Greg went over to his house for three straight evenings to do some repairs for him. It wasn't anything that needed immediate fixing, but Greg felt guilty about leaving his father and was trying to make it up to him."

Kay has another problem: Greg doesn't see his father in the same way she does. In fact, Greg thinks his father's demands are expressions of love and concern. Instead of telling Greg she doesn't like his father, therefore, Kay has opted for a more constructive approach. She has emotionally disengaged herself from her father-in-law. She refuses to feel responsible for fulfilling his every wish. When she is with him, she treats him with respect. Yet for the most part, she tries to avoid him. She doesn't go with Greg every time he visits his father. She doesn't talk to her father-in-law on the telephone any longer than is necessary to be courteous.

In addition, Kay says little to Greg about her father-in-law. Greg is aware that Kay doesn't feel close to his father. He doesn't understand why, of course. But the lack of closeness doesn't bother him because Kay is always kind and considerate toward her father-in-law.

Kay is practicing loving honesty. She treats her father-in-law well. However, she doesn't tell Greg everything. She doesn't share her assessment of her father-in-law with Greg. Kay doesn't feel that she can't tell Greg. Rather, she chooses not to tell him because at this point it would only hurt Greg. Perhaps in the future, Greg will begin to see his father more clearly. If so, Kay and Greg may have a different conversation about him.

Loving honesty requires the efforts of both spouses. As we pointed out, Greg is aware that Kay doesn't feel close to his father. Greg loves his father deeply. He also loves Kay deeply and knows that his first loyalty is to Kay. So he also is practicing loving honesty by not insisting that Kay talk about her feelings for his father.

Greg could make it very difficult for Kay by insisting that she tell him exactly how she feels about his father and why. He could, if he wished, force her to reveal her true feelings in order to avoid lying. He has chosen the wiser path of letting Kay handle the situation as she feels best.

The practice of loving honesty can be difficult or impossible if one spouse says things like, "I want you to tell me exactly what you are thinking about at this moment" or "I want you to tell me exactly how you feel about the outfit I'm wearing" or "I want to know precisely what you think about me as a lover" and so forth.

Frequently we make these kinds of statements out of uncertainty or insecurity. Rather than insist on the exact content of our spouse's mind, then, we could say, "I'm not sure if this is the best outfit for me; what do you think?" or "I want to be a good lover for you; how can I improve?" Phrasing questions in such form will not only enable our spouse to be more at ease in responding, but will achieve what we really need—help from someone who loves us.

You and your spouse need to help each other practice loving honesty. You can covenant with each other to accept the following principles:

1. Love means I trust you to be honest with me.
2. Love means I will be honest with you.
3. Love means I do not expect you to tell me everything you feel or think; I trust you to respect and support me.
4. Love means I respect your right to, and need for, a private part of your life; I trust you to share with me whatever is essential for the well-being of our relationship.

Notice carefully what these principles are saying. They do not say that you never encourage your spouse to share thoughts and feelings. Rather, they say that you will not press each other or insist that the other be transparently honest about something simply to satisfy your curiosity or personal need to know. The four points are designed to put the focus on your relationship rather than on your individual needs and desires.

CHANGE HONESTY

The second type of loving honesty, *change honesty*, also focuses on the relationship rather than individual needs. In essence, change honesty is acting or speaking differently in order to become the kind of person God wants you to be. Some Christians also may see change honesty as a form of deceit, even though the outcome of becoming that kind of person is to strengthen and enrich your marriage.

What You See Is What You Get

People are often attracted to the person who says, "What you see is what you get." It is a way of saying: "There's no deceit here, no guile. I am just what I appear to be." That, it would seem, is honesty.

Not always. Take the story of Scott and Molly. They are separated now after five years of marriage. We're not sure if they will get back together. This is Molly's perspective of their story. "Almost from the beginning, Scott has flirted with other women. He has embarrassed me by complimenting and ogling them in front of me. I know he has a reputation at work for being a ladies' man. He even flirts with women at church. It all came to a head for me when I went downtown one day to try to find him. I was going to surprise him and take him out to lunch. Instead, I found out that he had already gone. When I went to his usual spot for lunch, I found him holding the hand of one of his secretaries.

"I don't know if he has actually had an affair, but I'm a nervous wreck because I always suspect he might. If we don't make love for a few days, that's the first thing that comes into my mind: he's got another woman somewhere. I just can't go on living like this."

Here's Scott's perspective of their story. "I've never been

unfaithful to Molly. I tried to tell her that I was holding my secretary's hand because she was having big troubles in her marriage and I was trying to comfort her.

"It's true that I flirt a lot. But it's harmless. I wouldn't cheat on Molly. I just can't help flirting though. I love women. I told Molly that from the first time we met. That doesn't mean that I'll have an affair. But I'll go on flirting. It's just the way I am."

Is Scott practicing honesty? In a sense, yes. He is saying that what you see is what you get. He told Molly before they were ever married, "I fall in love with every woman I meet."

She assumed that this was an exaggeration and that, in any case, once they were married, he would no longer do it. "To show you how your thinking is muddled when you're in love," she said, "I even thought that made me someone special. He was in love with them all, but I was the one he wanted to marry."

To be sure, Molly did overreact to some of Scott's so-called flirtations. Scott *was* trying to console his secretary, although he didn't use good judgment in his method. In any case, he is correct in saying that he has always been honest with Molly about his feelings and his behavior.

But in another sense, Scott is practicing dishonesty. He is saying more than, "What you see is what you get"; he's also saying, "What you see is what you're always going to get. Accept me as I am because it's impossible for me to change."

Of course, that isn't true. Scott has choices. He can choose to practice change honesty, in which he starts behaving differently in order to become a different person. His response to that is a classic one: "But I can't help the way I feel." Is that true? Is Scott helpless to do anything about his feelings?

I Can't Help the Way I Feel

Most people assume that the way we behave is a reflection of the way we think and feel. That is, if I feel angry, I will behave angrily. If I feel lust for someone of the opposite sex, I will behave like a lecher. Most people also agree that we can't control such feelings.

The relationship between our feelings and our behavior is a rather complex one. Long ago the noted American psychologist and philosopher William James argued that we actually reverse the relationship. He said that we don't rant and rave because we are angry; rather, we feel angry because we are ranting and raving. We don't run because we are afraid; we are afraid because we are running away.

William James' argument seems to run counter to common sense and experience. Yet part of what he says is true. It isn't necessarily true that all our emotions are created by our behavior rather than vice-versa. It is true, however, that each can create the other. That is, just as our feelings can lead to certain kinds of behavior, we can create certain feelings by behaving in a certain way.

We can see an illustration of this truth in some research done with people watching cartoons. The researchers told half the people to smile while they looked at the cartoons, and they told the other half to frown while they looked at the same cartoons. The people were told to rate each cartoon according to how funny they found it. Those who smiled while looking at them found the cartoons much more humorous than did the other group.

Other research has shown that you can affect your mood by the way you behave. Try a simple exercise. If you do not normally smile throughout the day, put a smile on your face. You may have to keep working at it throughout the day. The payoff is worth the effort: if your smile persists, you will probably feel better at the end of the day.

Try another exercise. This one is based on some advice a saintly woman once gave us. "Is there anyone you don't like?" she asked us one day. "Do something nice for that person. You can't do something nice for someone and continue to dislike them." She was, of course, making very practical the Lord's teaching to love our enemies. It's another case of changing feelings by changing behavior.

Is it evident what all this has to do with Scott and Molly? Keep in mind that "behavior" includes our words as well as our actions. One of the ways that Scott could change, then, is to modify his behavior. He falls in love with every woman he meets because he *acts* as if he has fallen in love with every woman he meets. His words and body language both clearly say, "I am greatly attracted to you."

How could he change his behavior? He need not stop issuing compliments, of course. But consider the nature of his compliments. Once, when he and Molly were at a party, he was introduced to a young woman to whom he said, "Hi. What a pleasure. You know, you have the most beautiful eyes I've ever seen." He could have confined his remarks to something like, "It's nice to meet you. Have you met my wife, Molly?"

Furthermore, as he spoke to the young woman, he leaned toward her and looked deeply into her eyes. He could have extended his hand, but leaned toward or put his arm around Molly to show his commitment to her.

Would such measures change Scott's feelings? Certainly he would not experience an immediate and dramatic change in the way he feels, but we believe that his feelings would begin to alter. He would be constantly affirming his love and loyalty to Molly. As his feelings for Molly deepened, he would increasingly find her more attractive than other women.

This technique of affecting your feelings by controlling your behavior is an old one. We find it in Jesus' teaching: "For where your treasure is, there your heart will be also" (Matt. 6:21). It is important to note that Jesus did *not* say that we would put our treasure (the behavior) where our heart is (the feeling). Quite the opposite. Put your treasure in heaven, and your heart will follow.

The technique is also implied in the most common New Testament word for love, *agape.* As Greek scholars have pointed out, *agape* focuses more on the will than on feelings. To love people in a New Testament sense is to will to act in behalf of their well-being independently of whatever feelings you have for them. When you do that, however, your feelings will come into line with your behavior.

Some people may ask, "If I behave in a way that I don't feel, am I being deceitful?" As Scott said, "What am I supposed to do, pretend to be something that I'm not? That would be hypocritical." Would it? Let's look at that objection closely.

Becoming What God Wants You to Be

Every committed Christian wants to become what God wants him or her to be. One of the values of a Christian marriage is that you can help each other in that quest. And part of fulfilling that quest is to engage in change honesty. It is to do what Scott said would be hypocritical: pretend to be something that you are not. Or, more accurately, it is to act like the person you are becoming.

Let's look at an example of change honesty and then explain why this isn't hypocritical. Carl and April have been married three years. Carl developed the habit, learned from his father, of teasing people by making what he regarded as funny remarks about them. For Carl, as for his father, that frequently meant remarks that others regarded as sarcastic, caustic, or demeaning. For instance, Carl teased April by publicly joking about her supposed lack of intelligence (something he did not believe), particularly in matters that he regarded as his own domain. For example, he would say things like, "April can't balance a checkbook. She thinks that if your check bounces and the bank returns it, you've just got that much more to spend."

April didn't write the checks, so it wasn't her job to balance the checkbook. Carl was just engaging in what he thought was good fun. Their friends would chuckle, and April would smile indulgently. Admittedly, Carl had always teased her, even when they were dating. Yet he did it only when they were with other people. After they were married, they started going places with other married couples, and Carl's teasing also increased measurably.

April grew more uncomfortable with the situation and finally decided to talk to Carl about it. "It was hard to know what to say, because I knew he wasn't intentionally malicious. I told him that I knew he didn't really feel that way about me but that I was still embarrassed and a little hurt when he said such things in front of our friends. And I told him I thought he sometimes went too far in teasing them as well."

Carl was upset. He thought of himself as a faithful Christian husband and friend. When he calmed down, however, and reflected on what April had said, he admitted that she was right. He said he was grateful to April for the way she told him: "calmly and gently, as if she was making a request and not a demand."

Carl decided to change. For a while he became more quiet when they were with friends. He realized that most of what came into his mind were the kind of sarcastic, teasing remarks that he had always made. He also acknowledged that sometimes his caustic humor was a way of avoiding discussions of things about which he was sensitive or uncomfortable as well as a way of keeping people at a distance.

It took a while, but Carl is a different person now. Caustic remarks seldom even come into his mind. He has noticed that his friends seem much closer to him than before. Perhaps it's because he's no longer using humor to avoid talking about things that really matter to him; perhaps it's also a silent acknowledgment that his sarcastic remarks had sometimes bothered them also. And his marriage is stronger than ever.

Was Carl hypocritical when he didn't voice the sarcastic things that crossed his mind? Was he hypocritical to appear to be more kind in his attitudes and speech than he actually was? Not at all. He was engaging in change honesty, for he was being honest about the kind of person he wanted to become.

The difference between change honesty and hypocrisy, then, is one of motivation. Why do you behave as you do?

The person who harbors caustic thoughts but speaks with kind and flattering words to hide his or her true nature is hypocritical. The person who harbors caustic thoughts but speaks with kind words to become a kinder person according to the will of God is engaging in change honesty.

Change honesty is the practice of *agape*. Note that the Bible doesn't tell us to *feel* good about our enemies but to *do* good to them. The Bible doesn't tell us to feel affection for them but to pray for them. The biblical emphasis is on behaving appropriately. When we do, our feelings will gradually change, and we will become the kind of people that the behavior suggests we are.

We want to warn you that you are engaging in true change honesty only if you really want to change. For instance, if Carl had stopped his caustic remarks only to appease April, he would not have been honest with her. If Scott had stopped flirting with other women only when Molly was present, he would not have been honest with her.

Change honesty is a commitment to the following set of principles:

1. I want to become the kind of person God wants me to be.
2. Becoming the kind of person God wants me to be will also enable me to have the most rewarding kind of marriage.
3. In becoming the kind of person God wants me to be, I will sometimes have to act in a way that I don't feel like acting.
4. When I am acting contrary to my feelings and inner thoughts, I will pray that God changes me, and I will persevere until I become a different kind of person.

Some people may see your loving honesty as a form of deceit. But we believe that loving honesty is biblical and that it is the only kind of honesty that can bring a full and satisfying marriage.

Part IV

Building an Honest Relationship

Therefore encourage one another and build each other up.

1 THESSALONIANS 5:11

CHAPTER 11

Apples of Gold in the Home

*D*id you hear the story about the life-insurance salesman who was trying to sell a policy to a farmer? The salesman looked the farmer in the eye and said, "How will your wife carry on if you should die?" The farmer reflected a moment, then replied, "Well, I reckon that isn't any of my business, as long as she behaves herself while I'm still alive."

The story illustrates the difficulty, sometimes indeed the agony, of trying to communicate our meaning clearly to another person. Consider all the ways in which a message can get distorted. Let's say you wish to tell your spouse how you feel about your family's spending patterns. First, you may not even be entirely clear in your own mind how you feel. Second, you may have difficulty putting your feelings into words. Moreover, once you have expressed your feelings in words, you may not have chosen the best words or enough of them to convey completely how you feel. Third, when your spouse hears your words, he or she may attribute different meanings to them than you intended.

"When I use a word," Humpty Dumpty said in Lewis Carroll's *Through the Looking Glass,* "it means just what I choose it to mean—neither more nor less." He was wrong.

We would all like our words to mean exactly what we choose them to mean. We would all like to speak and be perfectly understood.

While talking is easy, communication is a complicated process. *Effective* communication is not only complicated but difficult; it is also essential for building an honest marriage. You can't be honest with your spouse unless you are able to communicate effectively how you think and feel about things. Furthermore, you can't be honest with each other unless you are able to understand clearly how your spouse thinks and feels.

Effective communication, then, is both an invaluable and an essential resource. As the Bible says: "A word aptly spoken is like apples of gold in settings of silver" (Prov. 25:11). In this chapter, we want to focus on ways to get more apples of gold into the home.

HIS TALK AND HER TALK

In the play *My Fair Lady*, Henry Higgins sings a song that expresses his bewilderment about women. Why, he wonders, can't they be more like men? Professor Higgins doesn't understand women, and he particularly doesn't understand why they act and react differently from his male friends.

Henry Higgins illustrates one of the fundamental problems in marital communication: many married couples have difficulty with communication because they are unaware of basic differences in the way men and women talk.

For instance, one man complained that his wife constantly wanted to talk about their relationship. "Our relationship is fine," he said. "The only thing I know is wrong is that she wants to keep talking about it." He was unaware that his wife was talking to him in a female conversational style.

Conversational Styles

Men's and women's conversational styles are both similar and different. We will focus on the differences here because they are likely to impede effective communication.

1. Women tend to ask more questions than men do. In conversations between professional couples, observers note that women asked three times as many questions as men.

2. Women use more "tag" questions, that is, questions at the end of a sentence to encourage the listener to respond. For example, "This is the right direction, isn't it?" and "We need to start saving more, don't you think?" are tag questions.

3. Women use more qualifiers, such as "sort of" and "maybe," and more intensifiers, such as "really." The husband who complained that his wife always seemed to hedge on everything she said didn't realize that what he heard from her simply reflected a female conversational style.

4. Men talk less than women do about personal matters. A psychiatrist has pointed out that, among other things, this means that women tend to believe that a marriage is working as long as they and their husbands can keep talking about it. Men, on the other hand, may think that a marriage is not working properly if they have to keep talking about it.

5. Men are more likely than women to make decisions without discussing the matter with their spouses.

6. Women tend to listen and give support; men tend to lecture and give authoritative information and opinions.

7. Women find details about daily activities to be a sign of intimacy and caring; men may find such details boring or even irritating. A husband may think or even say, "What's the point?" while his wife is going over details of her day. For her, the point is obvious: She is expressing that she cares about him, and she is building intimacy.

These differences in conversational styles reflect what communications expert Deborah Tannen calls basic differences in male-female approaches to life. She points out that men approach life as a contest in which each person is working to maintain independence and avert failure. Women, by contrast, approach life as a community affair in which the goal is to maintain intimacy and avoid isolation. Conversations tend to reflect these diverse approaches to life. Take the fifth point above as an example: When a woman talks with her spouse before making plans for her day, it may make her feel good because it indicates her life is intertwined with someone else's. On the other hand, for a man to discuss the matter with his spouse first may make him feel that he has lost his independence.

Do the Styles Enslave Us?

Much misunderstanding and conflict can occur in marriage simply as a result of the differing conversational styles of men and women. In fact, we were discussing some of these differences in a class when a woman said, "I realize something awful. I divorced my husband just because he was a *man*. I thought that he was being obstinate and insensitive to my needs. Now I see that he was just being typical. I think I need help in learning how to deal with men."

All men and all women need to learn how to deal with each other if they are going to build satisfying marriages. The differences in conversational styles mean that marriage in general—and an honest, fulfilling marriage in particular—is a challenge. The differences do not, however, mean that an honest, fulfilling marriage is an unrealizable ideal.

These differing styles are not built into our genes. For some men and some women, the styles we have described are reversed. In some cases, for instance, the husband is the one who listens and gives support, while the wife offers authoritative opinions. Or both husband and wife may have the style of the typical male or of the typical female. Most men and women fit into the styles we have described. The point is, the exceptions show that these are not inexorable and unchangeable male-female styles.

Developing a New Style

The God who makes all things new can also help us develop a conversational style that will nurture honesty in our discussions. Here are some guidelines that we believe will be useful:

1. Review the differences in male-female conversational styles. Think about them in terms of how you and your spouse tend to talk with each other.

2. Discuss together how you would like the other to grow, based on the above assessment. For example, the wife may say, "I would like you to talk with me more about personal matters, about what you're thinking and feeling." The husband may say, "I would like you to be clearer and firmer in expressing your own opinions so I know just where you stand."

3. Commit to help each other develop or enhance the skills you have agreed are important to your relationship.

4. Practice your skills with both small talk and serious discussions. The most satisfied couples are those who regularly discuss not only the events of their day but also the momentous issues that arise.

5. Recognize and avoid the "terminators" of honest dialogue. These terminators are guaranteed to end honest conversation.

- *Ordering* is necessary at times with children, but it is likely to create fear, anger, resistance, or resentment with your spouse. "Stop doing that," "You have to," and "You must" are ordering phrases.
- *Moralizing* tells your spouse that he or she should feel guilty or morally inferior. "You ought not" and "You should" are moralizing phrases.
- *Lecturing* makes your marriage like a parent-child

relationship. Lecturing tends to lower the self-esteem of your spouse at the same time that it highlights your own superiority. Examples of lecturing responses include, "You will have to learn how to keep the house cleaner if you want to be a good wife" and "You will have to be more forceful at work and demand a raise if you are going to be a good husband."

- *Criticizing* also lowers self-esteem and can lead to ongoing conflict. "You're always so untidy," "You never do things right," and "You're so dumb when it comes to money matters" are examples of destructive criticizing.
- *Analyzing* attributes motivation to your spouse and makes you an amateur psychoanalyst. "You're doing that only to hurt me" and "You're smiling only to cover up your hostility" are two examples.

We call all of these responses "terminators" because they kill honesty in conversation and depress the quality of the marital relationship. Let's look at an example of how a terminator works. Your spouse has purchased something that you think you can't afford. After a short, spirited conversation, you order your spouse to put a hold on the check. Your spouse becomes indignant and refuses, and you are quickly involved in an argument. The issue now becomes one of a power struggle between the two of you. All hope of an honest conversation in which you explore and discover each other's thoughts and feelings is lost.

6. Always remember that effective communication not only requires sharing feelings and thoughts but also requires skills in listening and speaking. These topics are so crucial that we will devote a separate section to each.

LEARNING HOW TO SHARE FEELINGS

You can't have an honest relationship if one or both of you are regularly unaware of the feelings of the other. Yet many people, particularly men, have trouble expressing their feelings to anyone else. Gary still struggles with this. "I know that my marriage has suffered at times because I have been unable to tell my wife exactly how I feel about something. I'm ashamed to say that at times I have even lied to her because I couldn't tell her my feelings. I know that isn't honest, but I grew up in a home where we just didn't talk about our feelings. I've been uncomfortable all my life whenever I try to express them. Even saying 'I love you' to my wife makes me feel a little embarrassed."

Gary learned early in life that males were expected always to be strong and in control. If he expresses sentimental feelings like love, he feels that he is something less than a "true" man. If he expresses negative feelings like anger, he feels that he has lost control of the situation; he also feels guilty because, in his mind, a Christian is not supposed to get angry.

Fortunately, Gary's wife, Glenda, is an understanding and patient woman. She has helped him over the years to be more expressive of his feelings, both by talking about her own feelings and by persistently encouraging Gary to open up to her. "I can think of three reasons why I've done it. First, I don't have any trouble talking about my feelings. It isn't fair for Gary to understand me and me not to understand him. Second, I can't be intimate with someone whose feelings are a mystery to me. And third, Gary's feelings come through in the way he looks and the tone of his voice. He's expressing feelings whether or not he knows it. But I don't want to misinterpret those feelings. That could get us into a lot of trouble.

"So it's been hard work. And at times, I really have gotten weary of it. Yet it's been necessary for our marriage to survive. Gary is so much better than he used to be. And so is our marriage."

Feelings Are Always Expressed

Glenda made an important point: Gary expressed his feelings all the time, only he did it in nonverbal ways.

Glenda made another important point: If Gary didn't tell her what his feelings were, she would infer them from his nonverbal signals and that could be disastrous.

Let's look at a fictitious discussion that avoids any mention of feelings. The husband initiates it because he desires to have sexual relations with his wife more often. As our commentary in brackets illustrates, such conversations can go on endlessly without the couple ever directly discussing the real issue.

> **He:** "I think that women don't have as strong a sexual drive as men." [He is upset, but wants to avoid offending her. He knows she is frequently stressed from dealing with both her career and their family. He approaches the topic obliquely, hoping she will respond to his comment.]

> **She:** "I don't know why you would say that." [She notices a slight edge to his voice. She knows he desires sex more often, and she thinks this might be a personal complaint. But she isn't sure. She thinks that he needs to understand the strain of being both a mother and a career woman. Perhaps if he helped around the house more, she would have more energy and interest in sex. Yet she doesn't want to misinterpret and offend. Basically, they have a good marriage. She makes her response as short and as neutral as possible.]

> **He:** "I just think it's true." [He saw her mouth tighten when she replied. He interprets her nonverbal signal as a warning that pursuing the topic could lead to an argument. Even though her words indicate that she rejects the idea of a lower sex drive, her nonverbal cues warn him that this is an emotional topic. He also decides to be neutral.]

> **She:** "Well, I've got too much to do to talk about something silly like that." [Hearing a softening in his voice, she decides he is unwilling to confront the issue directly. This angers her. She opts to force him to cut off the discussion or get to the point. In case he wants to pursue it, she has opened the door to what she

regards as the crux of the problem—an inequity in household responsibilities.]

Picture him now shrugging and turning on the television while she goes to do the laundry. What could have been a fruitful discussion, one that would have honestly presented both of their grievances, goes nowhere because neither spouse would express any feelings to the other. If he had begun by talking about his own upset or if she would have acknowledged her anger and sense of inequity, they could have discussed the issue and built a more honest and satisfying relationship.

Note that even though neither talked about feelings, each knew that the other was experiencing some feelings. Each interpreted those feelings and responded accordingly. Neither was certain of truly understanding the other. The net result was that they dropped the subject, and both spouses continued to be bothered by it. At some point the issue is likely to erupt again. In fact, if they do not deal with their grievances openly and frankly, they could soon find their relationship in serious trouble. It happens all the time.

You Can Help Each Other Express Feelings

Glenda and Gary's story illustrates another important point: Spouses can help each other learn how to better express feelings. You and your spouse can do a number of things. First, if your spouse has difficulty talking about feelings, you can encourage him or her by saying such things as: "You seem angry today. Is anything bothering you?" or "It is important to me to know how you feel about this matter. I can't deal with it when I'm puzzled about your feelings."

Such verbal encouragement won't necessarily cause immediate and dramatic change, but it can gradually help your spouse to be more open with you. If you are the one who has difficulty talking about your feelings, ask your spouse to keep encouraging you with such statements.

Second, when your spouse does express feelings, be careful to reward the effort. Too often we discourage people to express their feelings because we respond inappropriately when they express negative feelings. We say, "Oh, you shouldn't feel that way." Instead of making your spouse feel humiliated or guilty for having the feelings, then, reward him or her. After you listen and discuss the feelings, say something like, "Thank you for telling me. It really helps me, and I can be of more help to you when I know how you feel about something." Each time your spouse shares feelings with you, express your appreciation in some way.

Third, try using the following marriage-enrichment exercise. Use it on a regular basis until you each can easily communicate your feelings to each other. Set aside a time when you can talk to each other for fifteen minutes or more. If possible, sit facing each other so that you can easily observe your spouse's nonverbal signals. At the beginning, choose one or more nonthreatening subjects and share your feelings with each other. Be sure that you each hear how the other *feels* and not just how the other *thinks* about the matter. Try to get a complete emotional picture rather than just a simple answer. Over time, you can move to subjects that are more difficult to talk about.

For example, you might start off by telling each other how you feel about the various foods you eat. Each select a food item and ask the other about his or her feelings. Thus, the wife may begin by asking the husband, "How do you feel about spinach?" The following conversation might ensue.

He: "I don't feel that spinach is all that good for you."

She: "You said 'feel,' but you really told me what you *think* about it. How do you *feel* about it?"

He: "I don't like it."

She: "What else?"

He: "I don't like the way it looks or the way it tastes or even the way it feels in my mouth."

She: "You're doing great. Anything else?"

He: "Whenever I look at it, I get a funny little feeling in my stomach, like my stomach is telling me to be sure and stay away from that stuff."

She: "Wonderful. Now you pick out a food for me to talk about."

Learning to talk about your feelings for such trivial matters can help you to talk about them for more important things. Gradually you can use the exercise to explore feelings about such matters as your household routine, your finances, the amount of affection you express to each other, your fears, your aspirations, and so on. Once each of you has learned to express fully your feelings during the exercise, you should find yourself doing the same in regular conversations with each other. Your marriage will be a far more honest one because you each will have a better understanding of the other.

LEARNING TO LISTEN

Psychiatrist Karl Menninger wrote in one of his books that listening may be even more important than talking, that listening is one of the most powerful and important techniques of effective interaction. Listening is a learned skill, however. You haven't truly listened to someone just because you have heard words. Listening means to understand and to act on the other person's position: "Listen to advice and accept instruction, and in the end you will be wise" (Prov. 19:20).

Indeed, we can't be effective at anything unless we have good listening skills. When God called Ezekiel, he told him, "Son of man, listen carefully and take to heart all the words I speak to you" (Ezek. 3:10). "Listen carefully" means to hear every word. "Take to heart" means to take the words seriously, ponder them, understand them, and act on them. It is a good prescription for marital interaction as well as our interaction with God.

Sometimes when a couple comes for marriage counseling, it quickly becomes evident that one of the major problems is that one or both have never learned to listen. In some cases, it's like listening to two monologues interspersed with each other. More commonly, however, it is one of the spouses who doesn't listen. In either case, the effects on the relationship are destructive.

Dishonest Listening

It is possible to pretend to listen to someone without actually doing so. Such dishonest listening can ruin a relationship. Ellen was engaged to be married, but she canceled the wedding when she discovered that her fiancé consistently failed to listen to her even while giving the appearance of doing so. "I realized how little attention he paid to me when I told him one day that my doctor wanted me to have another test after he had found some suspicious cells in my cervix. Mike just looked at me and smiled. I really exploded. I was scared to death. He apologized. He said he was worried about some problems at work. I began probing into other things I thought we had talked about. He couldn't remember half the things I had told him!"

Mike had been fortunate up to that point. He had developed the habit of looking at Ellen and smiling when she talked and he was thinking about something else. It had worked for some time only because Ellen had talked about positive, happy things like their wedding and life together. Ellen, in fact, thought she was marrying someone who was an excellent listener. It pleased her that when she talked to Mike, he looked at her and nodded and smiled.

When she realized that he not only was not listening but was also deceiving her by pretending to listen, she decided that their relationship would not work. She didn't want to marry a man who was not honest with her. "For a while, I thought I would help him to change. But then I thought that if he did that to me before we were married, what could I expect afterward? How could I trust him? Maybe if it had been something different, I wouldn't have felt so strongly about it. But that test was a matter of life and death to me. And all he could do was smile."

Mike's smile faded into a frown when Ellen told him she would not marry him. He tried to persuade her that his preoccupation with work only meant that he would be an excellent provider. But his dishonest listening habits killed the relationship.

Honest Listening

Honest listening is trying not only to hear but also to understand what the other is saying. It is doing whatever you can to help the other to express his or her thoughts and feelings and then to let the other person know that you understand.

Clearly, then, effective listening is a complex process. You can do a number of things to improve your listening skills.

1. Be active even while you're silent. We tend to think of listening as a passive activity. But effective listening is work; it has to be active. You have to look at your spouse and concentrate on what he or she is saying. You need to watch the nonverbal cues as well as listen to the words to interpret what your spouse is trying to communicate. It is also helpful to respond from time to time with such words as "I see," or "Yes, I think I understand," and with such encouraging nonverbal signals as a nodding of your head (as long as you're really listening).

2. Resist distractions. The distractions may be in the environment, such as noise in your home. Some people can talk and listen in spite of background noise. Others will need to find a place where they can be free of such distractions. The distractions may be inner distractions, such as a preoccupation with some problem or concern.

It was Mike's inability to deal with distractions that doomed his relationship with Ellen. One thing he could have done early on was to tell her that he was preoccupied and to ask her to repeat what she had said instead of pretending to hear and agree. Even better, he could have told her when they got together that he was bothered by something and asked to talk it out with her.

The point is, if you're distracted by something that is going through your mind, you may need to discuss it with your spouse instead of carrying on an internal dialogue with yourself. You can't build intimacy if you're barely aware of your spouse's presence.

3. *Control your emotions and your tendency to respond before your spouse is finished.* Another part of active listening is suppressing your tendency to interrupt. You may want to reply to certain points at once. Resist that. Hear your spouse out completely, even if you think that he or she will want to hear immediately your reply to a point. If your reply is really that good or that important, you won't forget it in the few minutes that it takes for your spouse to finish.

You will be particularly tempted to interrupt if your spouse pushes one of your hot buttons—some word or idea that creates an emotional reaction in you. Whenever someone says something that produces an emotional reaction in us, we tend to stop listening and start formulating a reply. For example, does the following conversation sound like something you have heard or experienced?

> **He:** "I really feel overwhelmed right now. I need about an extra twenty hours each week."
>
> **She:** "Maybe I can help. Tell me all you have to do, and let's see if I can take some of it off your hands."
>
> **He:** "I think you can. In fact, if you wouldn't have to go see your mother every week we could—"
>
> **She:** [angrily] "I'm not asking you to go. I need to go see Mom. I said I would help you, but I'm not going to stop seeing my mother."
>
> **He:** "I didn't say you had to *stop* seeing her. I only—"
>
> **She:** "Look, I know you don't like my mother. But she *is* my mother, and I'll see her as often as I want."

He: "Just forget it. I'll take care of what I have to do, and you take care of your mother."

Clearly, the subject of her mother is a touchy one. He would have been wise not to have mentioned it at that point. She would have shown good listening skills by not allowing it to push her hot button and by hearing him out instead. The net result is that he still has his problem of feeling overwhelmed, and they still have the problem of their contrary views about her visits with her mother.

It's difficult to continue to listen when someone says something that produces feelings of anger, anxiety, or humiliation. Nevertheless, it can be done. If you fail, give yourself another chance. In the scenario above, for example, one approach the wife could take is saying to her husband, "I'm sorry I blew up when you mentioned my mother. Let's talk about how I can help you. And then we'll talk about my visits to Mom as well."

4. *Ask questions, and rephrase your spouse's words to clarify meaning.* Not all questions are helpful. Some people use questions to cast suspicion on motives: "Are you saying that just to annoy me?" The effective listener, however, uses questions to get clarification: "Are you saying that you are really hurt because I was late?"

Effective listeners are particularly aware of the importance of rephrasing, which is done to clarify, to check for accuracy, to check for feelings, or simply to show interest and understanding. For instance, a husband might say to his wife, "We've shot our budget in the foot this month. You've got to stop spending so much money." His wife could respond with anger: "What about your spending habits? It's not all my fault." That sounds like the beginning of a spirited argument.

What if the wife responded like an effective listener (in spite of the husband's poor choice of words)? She might say, "You feel that our budget problems are due mainly to my spending habits?" (clarification) or "You're angry because of the way I spend money?" (checking for feelings).

This is an invitation to discuss the budget problem in a constructive way.

5. *Practice.* You can enhance your listening skills by practicing. Do it with everyone, not simply your spouse. You will find that the quality of your intimate relations generally will improve greatly to the extent that you are an effective listener. Moreover, the quality of your marriage will improve directly with every improvement you make in your listening skills.

An old Chinese tale describes a man who was humiliated by another and who replied, "I am much like you—a mouth carried between a couple of shoulders." The imagery is graphic. You probably know people to whom it applies. In contrast, the person who is building an honest, satisfying marriage always has two well-functioning ears as well as a mouth that is carried between the shoulders.

CHAPTER 12

Honest-to-Goodness Fighting

W e all can say with certainty two things about conflict in family life: Virtually no one likes it, and everyone experiences it.

Since nearly everyone dislikes it, we all want to eliminate it. Even if it were possible to do so, it would be a serious mistake. You can't have an honest marriage or an honest family life without conflict. Let's look at why this is true. Then we'll discuss some ways to make conflict a constructive rather than a destructive factor.

THE IMPORTANCE OF CONFLICT

Each of us has a particular style that we tend to use in conflict. You and your spouse may, for example, approach conflict as a kind of game in which the object is for one of you to win. You may view it as a disagreement that requires compromise. You may view it as a problem that needs to be solved. Or you may dislike conflict so much that you either give in after a short struggle or avoid it altogether. Depending on what style you tend to use, you could find yourself engaging mainly in either honest or dishonest conflict in your marriage.

Dishonest Conflict Erodes

If you always give in after a short struggle, if you avoid conflict altogether, or if you view it as a game to be won, you are engaging in dishonest conflict. It is dishonest because all of these styles require you to be secretive to some extent about your needs and views and aims.

Take, for example, the style of avoidance. It is an easy style to adopt because most of us dislike conflict. In addition, we may mistakenly believe that conflict avoidance is the Christian approach to relationships. If you feel that you are falling short of your Christian responsibility when you engage in conflict, remember that Jesus did battle with the Pharisees and that Paul confronted Peter over the issue of eating with Gentiles. Nothing in Scripture overtly condemns interpersonal conflict.

But why is avoidance dishonest? Listen to the following conversation, which is typical of those we frequently hear in marriage counseling:

She: "Whenever we have a fight, he tends to just clam up."

He: "I don't see any point in arguing."

She: "But if you don't tell me your side of the story, how am I to know what to do?"

He: "It doesn't help to argue."

She: "But then nothing ever gets resolved. Besides, you may not argue, but you sure do pout."

He: "I just don't like to argue."

She: "Well, call it something else then. Call it a heated discussion. Call it anything. But for heaven's sake, talk to me so that I can understand your point of view."

Note that this woman's main complaint is that she doesn't know her husband's perspective on the issue. And if she doesn't know how he thinks and feels about a problem, how can they resolve it? Even in the presence of the counselor, he has difficulty talking about his feelings about conflict. Little wonder that his wife is frustrated. Unfortunately, he may think that he is being a kind and considerate Christian by refusing to engage in conflict. However, he is only making the situation more troubled, for he is keeping secret something that is essential to resolving the problem: his own thoughts and feelings.

Furthermore, this husband is not really avoiding conflict. The term "avoidance" simply means a refusal to engage openly in conflict. He was not truly avoiding it, however, either for himself or his spouse. She fretted openly about his refusal to confront their difficulties; he, as she pointed out, pouted and was inwardly in turmoil about their problems. Ironically, then, so-called avoidance can simply be a way of prolonging the conflict or of avoiding a solution to the disagreement.

Similarly, if you view conflict as a game to be won, you will have to engage in a certain amount of deceit. People who take this approach generally are highly competitive. The only firm rule for a highly competitive person is this: Do what you have to do to win. You may have to withhold some information. You may have to mislead the other person. You may have to make claims that are false. No matter. The point is to win.

A young married couple told us not only about their arguments, but about their conflict over the way they argued! He accused her of resorting to the "silent treatment" when they were having trouble coming to a resolution, and using silence as a kind of unspoken victory. She accused him of wanting to win so badly that he would sometimes argue for a point that he himself didn't really believe. Both were right. And each eventually agreed that the other was right. They were two highly competitive people, and each was engaging in dishonest conflict in a determined effort to win.

Honest Conflict Clarifies

One of the reasons that conflict is necessary (note that we do not simply say useful) for an honest relationship is that conflict clarifies issues. Recall that when Peter came to Antioch, Paul "opposed him to his face," telling Peter, "You are a Jew, yet you live like a Gentile and not like a Jew. How is it, then, that you force Gentiles to follow Jewish customs?" (Gal. 2:15).

What if Paul had believed that controversy was wrong and said nothing to Peter? He would have continued to resent Peter's behavior, of course. No doubt he would have felt alienated from Peter because of that behavior. Yet the issue would have remained unresolved at least until something else forced the problem into the open.

Similarly, conflict in family life is an important way of clarifying disagreements. And it is only when you have clarified—when you each fully understand the position of the other—that you are able to resolve the problem.

Sometimes the clarifying conflict occurs after a period of annoyance. The annoyance finally erupts in an argument, and the ensuing conflict can then clarify for one or both spouses what has been going on. For instance, Ben and Lila have been married nine years and have had a normal amount of conflict. In a marriage-enrichment session, Lila shared an example of how conflict has helped them. "As I look back on it, it was kind of silly. But for years I would get aggravated when doing the laundry. I didn't know why. Or at least, I never gave it any thought. I just figured that no one likes to do laundry.

"One evening when I was working late on the laundry, I felt exhausted. I was turning Ben's socks right side out, and I just suddenly snapped at him. 'Why don't you turn your clothes right side out when you put them in the hamper?' I think he was rather startled. But he was tired and pretty sarcastic when he said, 'I don't think we have to be neat with dirty clothes.'

"We said a few other choice things to each other. Then I

realized that one of the reasons I was always aggravated was that his clothes were so tangled. I told him that it would really help me if he just turned his clothes right side out. He was still a little perturbed and said he didn't have the time to do that. Of course, this really rankled me; he sounded as if he was busier than I was and that his time was more valuable than mine. Well, after some discussion, he backed down and said he would be careful to do it from then on. It had never occurred to him that he was causing me extra work."

The brief conflict clarified the issue for both Lila and Ben. As Lila pointed out, it was during the conflict that she realized one reason the laundry had been annoying to her. It was also during the conflict that Ben saw a simple way he could help his wife. Many conflicts are not that brief and straightforward, but honest conflict does clarify issues.

Honest Conflict Solidifies

We tend to think of conflict as dividing people. Temporarily that can happen. However, honest conflict solidifies people over the long run. As one woman in a long-term marriage told us, "Of course we argue. Our marriage is worth fighting for."

Marriage counselors know that not every troubled marriage is marred by conflict. In some cases, the spouses may stay together and never argue, but their relationship has no life. They are not really involved with each other. The relationship is on a dead-end course, lacking vitality and true commitment. As one marriage counselor put it, the marriage is dying of dry rot.

One of the benefits of conflict is that it can prevent the dry rot that slowly corrodes a relationship. In a real sense, conflict is a refusal to let a relationship deteriorate. It is a way of saying to each other, "I care enough about you and about our relationship to fight for us."

If the conflict is honest (we will discuss the rules of honest conflict in the next section), the result will be a stronger, more satisfying relationship. At first glance, it may appear contrary to common sense to say that conflict solidifies a relationship. Yet consider some of the benefits that honest conflict can produce.

- You understand each other better than before.
- You have worked together to solve a problem.
- You have affirmed your commitment to each other by not allowing a disagreement to persist.
- You have demonstrated your respect for each other by hearing each other's point of view and finding a resolution that incorporates each other's point of view.
- You have affirmed your love for each other by not using the conflict to gain personal advantage.

You probably will not enjoy the conflict, but it can bring you many benefits if you handle it properly. Let's look closely, therefore, at what we mean by honest conflict.

THE RULES OF HONEST CONFLICT

Not all conflict clarifies and solidifies. Many marriages and many families have been torn apart by intense and incessant conflict. Conflict that is carried on poorly is destructive. On the other hand, honest conflict—conflict that clarifies and solidifies—follows a number of important rules.

Maintain Your Perspective

We have said that avoidance is a poor choice of conflict styles. Let us modify that slightly. At times avoidance is the most appropriate style because not everything is worth fighting about. As one man told us, "We don't treat every incident as if it's a disaster. I'm not by nature a fighter. But I will fight if I feel the issue is worth it. We would both rather make love than war. So if a disagreement comes up over, say, something like whether we should buy some new furniture, I tell her to go ahead even though I don't feel we need it. Why should we fight over a few dollars for furniture? Sometimes I give in, and sometimes she gives in. We just feel that most disagreements aren't as important as our good relationship."

Of course, we each have to decide for ourselves what is and what isn't worth fighting about. For some couples, money spent on furniture or other items may be more critical because of the budget. The point is not to identify in advance what is significant and what is trivial but to note that we all have both kinds of disagreements. The husband's advice is wise: don't fight over trivial things.

The other side of maintaining your perspective is to overcome your dislike of conflict and be willing to argue when one or both of you feel the matter is important. In other words, a proper perspective on conflict neither minimizes the importance of arguing when necessary nor falls into the trap of arguing about trivial things.

Develop Tension Outlets

Have you ever snapped at your spouse because you were frustrated by something that happened at work or in a store or in a telephone call? Sometimes conflict is the result of issues between spouses, and sometimes it results from outside frustrations. We live in an age of stress. This stress can affect your mood, and your mood can lead to arguments.

Ben and Lila, whom we spoke about earlier, provided another example of conflict for us. In this case, it was a situation that was dishonest and destructive until they faced it honestly. The conflict was rooted in an outside source of frustration. This is how they reported it.

Lila: "Sometimes we would have tense conversations that eventually turned into arguments. I knew Ben was upset when he got home, but I didn't know the reason. I would try to get him to talk about it, but he wouldn't."

Ben: "I've never believed in bringing my problems at work home with me. I don't want to impose them on Lila."

Lila: "But that was the point. You were imposing them on me anyway. And it was worse than imposing them because I wasn't sure if it was something at work or if it was me. It's important to me to know what's going on with you."

Ben: "I realize that now. I'm doing my best to talk about what happens at work and why I sometimes come home in a grouchy mood. However, it's still hard. My father never did that to my mother."

Lila: "That worked fine for them. But it won't work for us because I need to know what's bothering you. Your mother just ignored it and gave her attention to you kids. I can't do that."

Lila agreed that Ben is much better now. They seldom have arguments anymore because of Ben's work-induced mood. In part, that is because Ben is working on sharing his work life with Lila. In part, it is because Ben has been able to reduce the effects of his stressful work by finding a tension outlet; he now runs three miles a day. Since he started running, Ben says, "I have the same problems at work, but they don't get to me as much as they used to. Running is great therapy."

Everyone needs some kind of tension outlet. This minimizes the possibility that you will make your spouse the victim of the stresses you face each day. Regular exercise, like running, is one possibility. Other couples find other ways, from getting away together for periods of time to cultivating humor in their relationship. One woman told us that she looks for something humorous each day to share with her husband. "A laugh a day keeps the therapist away," she declared. For them, it also means that they are less likely to have conflict that arises from outside frustrations and tensions.

Avoid Festering Resentment

"'In your anger, do not sin': Do not let the sun go down while you are still angry, and do not give the devil a foothold" (Eph. 4:26—27). In that brief passage, Paul sums up some important counsel about anger. First, he recognizes that we will feel anger. Second, he reminds us not to nurture that anger but to get rid of it quickly.

How do you "nurture" anger? By refusing to express it or by avoiding a confrontation with the person with whom you are angry. You need not necessarily confront the person with whom you are angry in order to express your anger. For example, you may be angry with your boss, but you can't confront your boss because he or she doesn't understand and doesn't tolerate such a confrontation. You then need to talk about your anger and your situation with your spouse or with someone else you trust. Otherwise you may find yourself soured by festering resentment, and you may take out your anger on the people you love.

If your anger is with your spouse, on the other hand, it's wise to deal with it as quickly as possible. A husband talked about an early experience he had with his wife of nearly thirty years. "Shortly after we were married, we had a fight about something, and I went to bed angry and frustrated. I don't remember what the argument was about. But I remember very well lying in the dark and seething on the inside. Suddenly, Betty began to whistle. I said, 'What in the world are you doing?' She told me that she didn't think we should go to sleep while we were angry. She believed in Paul's advice to the Ephesians. So we turned on the lights and worked it out. It's a great rule to follow."

To be sure, not every disagreement can be worked out in a short time. We are certainly not suggesting that you refuse to sleep or to allow your spouse to sleep before you have solved every problem that arises in your marriage. However, you can usually deal with the anger even though you haven't completely solved the problem. Just knowing that both of you are committed to solving the problem can ease the anger.

Use Conflict to Attack Problems, Not Your Spouse

A fundamental rule of honest conflict is to keep the focus on the problem. This means to take the approach of "we have a problem" and not "you are the problem." The fifteenth chapter of Acts describes the Council at Jerusalem, which was called to deal with the question of whether circumcision was necessary for Christian salvation. Many people held differing opinions and were involved in "much discussion" before Peter stood up to affirm God's acceptance of Gentiles without circumcision (Acts 15:7–11). In the entire account, we hear people addressing the problem; not once does the record indicate a personal attack on another Christian.

You and your spouse can do two things to keep the focus on the problem and avoid attacking each other. One is to decide at the outset that the conflict is a disagreement over some issue rather than a personal attack on yourself. Even if your spouse criticizes something you say or do, you need to distinguish between an attack on some habit and an attack on you as a person.

One husband told us that it took him a number of years to be able to make the distinction. "When my wife would correct my eating habits, I thought she was despising me as a person. When she glared at me for something I had said, I thought she was showing her disgust for me as a person. One day I realized that she only did those things because she loved *me*, even though she didn't like some of the things I did."

The second thing you can do is to avoid hurting your spouse. Sometimes an argument degenerates into a mutual-insult session. Each spouse makes a series of derogatory statements about the other. Your conflict need not sink to such a level. To avoid saying hurtful things, however, you may need to be careful about your emotional state, which leads us to the next principle.

Argue Only When You Can Control Your Emotions

The great majority of the 300 happy couples in our research of long-term marriages agreed that conflict must be carried on with relative calmness. "Don't fight while your emotions are at a fever pitch," said a wife. "Make sure that you can discuss the problem with your mind as well as your emotions," a husband advised.

It's important to understand exactly what we are saying here. We are *not* saying that your arguments must be devoid of emotion or raised voices. It is difficult to imagine Jesus cleansing the temple of the money-changers or Paul confronting Peter about the latter's inappropriate treatment of Gentiles in a perfectly calm voice.

The point is not that you will express no emotions in your disagreements. The point is that your emotions will not overrule your mind and control what you say and how you act during the conflict. In premarital counseling, we suggest to couples that a good test of whether you are ready to engage in conflict is whether you can be an observer as well as a participant in the discussion. It is possible to do both. As an observer, you note what your spouse is saying as well as what feelings he or she is expressing. You monitor what you say. As an observer, you make sure that you are staying within the bounds of the various rules we are discussing in this section.

If you are not able to observe and control what you say, if your emotions are so intense that they are likely to drive you to say things and to act in ways that are destructive, then you should not engage in the conflict until your emotions have subsided somewhat.

For example, if your emotions are intense, you may say something that you know will hurt your spouse. And one of the dangers in an intimate relationship is that we get to know very well the other person's vulnerable spots. This means that no one knows how to hurt you more than your spouse. Yet, as we pointed out, conflict should always be used to attack the problem, not the spouse. If a part of you is observing the conflict, you should be able to control what you say and avoid attacking your spouse. You need not let your emotions mar your relationship.

But what if you have your emotions under control and it is your spouse who is driven by emotion? Then remember the counsel of Proverbs: "A gentle answer turns away wrath, but a harsh word stirs up anger" (Prov. 15:1). If you respond angrily to anger, it is like trying to douse a fire with gasoline. If you respond calmly to anger, however, you can usually quiet the anger of your spouse. Then you both are in a better position to attack the problem in constructive ways.

Watch the Timing of Your Conflict

Politicians and athletic teams know the importance of timing. You can "peak" too soon or too late in terms of your optimal performance. Only if you peak at just the right time are you likely to emerge the victor.

Timing is also important in marriage. In terms of conflict, timing means that there are good and poor times to engage in an argument. We noted earlier that you should not nurture your anger, but you should instead express it. However, this doesn't necessarily mean that you express it at the first opportunity. Suppose, for example, that you are angry about something that happened yesterday. You had not been able to resolve the anger last night, and you had no time to deal with it in the morning. You and your spouse come home from a long day's work, and both of you are exhausted. In spite of the anger, it may be better to wait until you have eaten and relaxed a bit before bringing up the problem again. None of us deals effectively with conflict when we are weary or hungry.

It's also not wise to deal with conflict when you are with other people, when you enter a restaurant or other public place, or just before an important meeting. These may sound so commonsensical that they hardly merit attention. Yet we have known people who consistently violate them. Early in our own marriage, we had some friends with whom we frequently dined. Most of the times we were together, they would manage to start arguing with each other about one matter or another. It made the meals most uncomfortable for us. Eventually we simply stopped going out with them.

Continue to Communicate

To continue to communicate means, first, that the so-called silent treatment is taboo for Christians. Some people think that the silent treatment means you have stopped communicating. It doesn't. It is, in fact, a very powerful form of communication. It communicates anger, scorn for the other, a refusal to negotiate, a desire to hurt, and whatever else it may mean to the victim. In short, the silent treatment is an excellent way to prolong and intensify conflict.

On the other hand, just because you are talking to each other doesn't mean that you are communicating effectively. Have you ever tried to argue with someone who can only keep repeating the same complaint? It can sound like this:

He: "I don't understand why you're so cold."

She: "You really hurt me."

He: "I didn't mean to. Let's get beyond this."

She: "But you really hurt me."

He: "Well, what can I do to make it up to you?"

She: "I don't know. You really hurt me."

In other words, the *kind* of communication is as important as the bare fact of communication. In a conflict situation, you are communicating effectively when

- each of you articulates how you feel and think about the issue.

- each of you is confident that the other understands how you feel and think.
- each of you is willing to discuss ways to resolve the issue in the light of your mutual feelings and thoughts.

Such communication demands effective listening, as we described it in the last chapter. It is hard to listen to someone when you are upset. You may be so eager to express your own point of view that you are only barely hearing your spouse. Role reversal is an effective technique to help each of you truly listen to the other. In role reversal, each of you takes the role of the other and expresses the other's point of view and feelings.

For example, let's say that you are having a dispute about the proper way to discipline your children. At some point, one of you can say, "Let's see if we really understand each other. I'll argue this from your perspective, and you argue it from mine." Each of you then has the opportunity to correct your spouse if he or she has a faulty understanding.

Role reversal has another rather subtle benefit. In arguing your spouse's position, you may find that it has more merit than you realized. Your spouse may come to the same conclusion about your position. If so, it should be easier for you to find an acceptable resolution. In any case, simply making sure that each of you fully understands the other will facilitate the process of working through the disagreement.

Stay Flexible, Open to Compromise

The term "compromise" has an unpleasant ring for many of us. We have heard about the dangers of "compromising" our Christian beliefs or ethics. We have no doubt experienced a compromise that was less than what we would have preferred in a particular situation.

However, compromise is one of God's gifts to us. In

fact, one could say that God taught us the art of compromise when he bargained with Abraham over the number of righteous people that could save Sodom (Gen. 18:22–33) and when he allowed Ezekiel to bake his food on animal rather than human dung as God had first commanded (Ezek. 4:9–15).

Don't think of compromise, then, as giving in to something less than the ideal but rather as a realistic way to handle differences. After all, few of our differences involve moral questions that involve clear-cut, right or wrong positions. Most are judgment calls or a matter of preference.

Arguments over money, for instance, are rarely about whether to give a portion of one's income to the Lord's work. Rather, the arguments are about how much to spend and how much to save, whether to buy one product or another, or whether one spouse is a spendthrift (in which case, the other is probably viewed as a tightwad). Such arguments boil down not to right or wrong but to preferences and values and upbringing.

Carla and Russell have had five years of good marriage in every way except one: they have ongoing arguments about finances. In listening to them, we could see that each believed there was a right and wrong way to handle their finances and that each of their views came from the way they were raised.

Carla grew up in a family that stressed thrift. Her father never bought anything on credit except their home. He even paid cash for his cars. Her mother never went on a shopping spree. Presents at Christmas and on birthdays were simple and few.

In contrast, Russell grew up in a family that had few rules about spending. His father and mother each would come home at times with something they had bought on impulse. Presents abounded at Christmas and on birthdays. They were always heavily in debt, but they seemed undisturbed by that fact. Money, they liked to say, was to be spent, not hoarded.

Conflict over money was almost a given for two people

raised in such different backgrounds, particularly since each of them accepted the values of their parents. Carla and Russell are now working on their differences. Clearly, any resolution must involve a compromise for both of them. They must first recognize that neither family's practice was right or wrong, just different. "The way Russell can freely spend money just seems *wrong* to me," Carla admits. She is working on seeing it as different rather than wrong and on seeing Russell's need to have some money he can freely spend.

Russell also has to change his understanding. "Carla can be so tight with our money that we can't do anything. What's the point of saving everything?" Russell is working on understanding Carla's need to see a certain amount of money regularly going into savings accounts. Carla and Russell are just about at a point of agreement as to how much each month can be used as Russell wishes and how much will be put into a savings account. Their compromise requires a negotiation of amounts, but the negotiation could not proceed until each was flexible enough to change perspectives on the other's way of dealing with money.

Continue to Love While Fighting

Love and fight at the same time? They may sound like contradictory activities, but you can continue to love even while you are engaged in conflict. Keep in mind that *agape* is not a feeling but a behavior, a behavior that expresses concern for the well-being of the other independently of your own feelings at the moment.

But exactly how do you continue to love your spouse while you are in conflict with him or her? We have already mentioned one way that love is practiced in an argument: Love refuses to say anything or do anything that will hurt the other.

Another way to love is to keep in mind what you like about your spouse. As one wife told us, "I believe you can let your husband know you still love him even though the two of you disagree about something. When we're having a fight, I try to focus on my husband's good points, on the things I like about him rather than on his negative qualities. I think it gets through to him that I am still loving him even while we're fighting. At least it seems to help us resolve our arguments."

You can do this if you keep in mind what we discussed above—the need to engage in conflict only when you can be an observer as well as a participant. As an observer, you can look at your spouse while arguing and recall some of the things that led the two of you to get married or some of the qualities that you value in your spouse. It is likely that such thoughts will come through in your tone of voice and looks. As the wife quoted above said, it should help you to resolve your arguments.

Finally, if you have kept loving your spouse during the conflict, you are more likely to reap the benefits of honest fighting. Your conflict will not smudge your relationship. Rather, it will clarify and solidify your marriage.

CHAPTER **13**

Speaking the Truth in Love: The Bridled Tongue at Work

Francine has had many painful experiences with transparent honesty in her marriage, but one of the most damaging occurred about six months after her wedding. She and her husband, Hank, an Air Force officer, moved far away from family and friends immediately after their wedding. She says that being so far away from home increased her desire to become the "perfect" wife to Hank. "I was determined to please him in every way. I wanted to be the best homemaker, the best cook, and the most efficient manager possible—all wrapped up in a loving, attractive package. No doubt about it, I set high standards for myself."

Unfortunately, Hank didn't seem to appreciate Francine's hard work and efforts to please him. In fact, often he didn't even notice her best attempts and seemed to take all of her hard work for granted. Francine resented his inattention but excused it because "he was so very busy and preoccupied with his career."

Major difficulties developed, however, on Hank's birthday—the first one they had celebrated together as husband and wife. "I wanted everything to be perfect. It took me weeks to find the ideal gift, a new set of golf clubs. He had just started playing the game and was constantly mentioning how much he wanted his own clubs. I also planned his favorite meal—steak, baked potato, and asparagus. To top it off, I made a Black Forest cake. It was the first time I had tried such an adventurous and demanding dessert, but I was pleased with the way it turned out.

"I had everything ready when he came home from the base. You can't imagine how excited I was. My pleasure didn't last for long, however. When Hank opened my gift, he seemed irritated instead of pleased. He finally told me he thought the gift was too expensive (even though I had bought it on sale), and these weren't the golf clubs he wanted anyway. After seeing the hurt look on my face, he simmered down. And I hoped that all was not lost. Surely, he would be impressed with the meal.

"Well, was I wrong. He complained that the steak was too tough and that I didn't have real butter for the potato. But the most awful moment came when I brought in the birthday cake. His reaction was, 'What happened to the cake? It's lopsided.' And 'Why did you make a cake with cherries anyway? I hate cherries.' That was the final straw. I was devastated. I loved Hank so much and wanted his birthday to be a memorable occasion. Well, it was memorable; even after thirteen years, I still remember how much his words hurt."

It's not surprising that Hank and Francine have had a troubled marriage. The combination of Hank's disregard and painful criticism eroded their relationship until it was almost beyond repair. By the time they finally came for counseling, Francine had stored up so many bitter memories and was so resentful of Hank that reconciliation seemed unlikely.

Interestingly enough, when Francine confronted Hank in counseling sessions with the hurtful things he had said to her over the years, his response was, "I didn't intend to hurt you; I was just honestly telling you what I thought and felt." But his words, no matter how honest, caused deep damage to Francine and to their relationship. And the damage has been so great that three years of counseling have not yet healed their marriage.

No question about it, transparent honesty has nearly wrecked Francine and Hank's marriage. The situation would have been very different if Hank had practiced monitored honesty, which we discussed in chapter 10. Monitored honesty follows the biblical injunctions to speak the truth in love and to keep a rein on our tongues.

Monitored honesty builds and nurtures relationships. But it's not always easy to practice. How do you walk the fine line between monitored and transparent honesty? How do you know when to speak and when not to speak? When is it appropriate or inappropriate to share your thoughts and feelings with your spouse? And how much do you share with him or her? In particular, we are talking about the kinds of thoughts and feelings that can be disruptive in some way to your relationship. For instance:

- Should you talk to your spouse about some annoying habit that he or she has?
- Should you tell your spouse if you have had an affair or if you have been tempted to have an affair?
- Should you reveal your feelings when you feel strong dislike or contempt for your spouse?
- Should you talk about the times you think you'd like to be single again?
- Should you speak up if you think your spouse is inept at something or is behaving inappropriately in public?

Such questions do not have quick and easy answers. Moreover, it's important to keep in mind that the same question might receive a different answer depending on the circumstances in which it is asked. So how do you know what to do? Ask yourself these four questions to help you make a decision.

QUESTION 1: WHY DO I WANT TO SHARE THIS?

First, you need to be honest with yourself and answer the question of why you want to share it. You may find you have various motives: you may feel guilt, you may be irritable, or you may just want to connect.

"I Feel Guilty"

Recall the story of Dan and Sharon in the first chapter. When Dan reflected on why he had told Sharon about his attraction to one of his students, he had to admit that he had mixed motives. But clearly one of his motives was that he wanted to relieve his own sense of guilt.

Sometimes you should confess feelings of guilt to your spouse. When you have said something hurtful or when you have subjected your spouse to the silent treatment or when you behaved in a way that seriously distressed your spouse, it is appropriate to confess feelings of guilt. "I feel bad about the way I talked to you yesterday" or "I feel guilty because I ignored you when you wanted to make love" or "I feel terrible because I put you down in front of our friends" are appropriate expressions of guilt.

It can also be appropriate to confess feelings of guilt about outside matters: "I don't think my behavior was right at work today; I certainly didn't act like a Christian" or "I told the teacher that John always does his homework, but I know that he sometimes doesn't" or "The clerk gave me too much change back, but I just kept it." Spouses can help each other decide what to do as Christians in a variety of situations. Under such circumstances, sharing something for which you feel guilty is not only appropriate but one of the benefits of a Christian marriage.

Yet as the case of Dan and Sharon illustrates, to share something with your spouse simply because you feel guilty can be a disaster rather than an appropriate Christian procedure. In fact, Sharon said that it was harder for her to forgive Dan for telling her than for having the feelings about the student. Before sharing something out of a sense of guilt, then, you need to answer the other questions we pose in this chapter.

"I Feel Irritable/Weary/Disgusted/Frustrated"

We all have periods of being in a negative mood. The moods come from a variety of sources, including feelings of being over-worked, under-appreciated, pressured by time, bored by too much routine, hassled by finances, and so on. When we're in such moods, we may speak things that we ordinarily would not and should not say.

For instance, Terry has been married thirty-six years, but he can still recall an incident that happened early in his marriage, an incident that taught him the importance of learning to bridle his tongue. "I was in a snit. I think it was just all the pressures I was going through at work, but I was in a snit. Everything and everyone irritated me. My wife and I were driving to her parents' house to pick up our two kids. Unfortunately for her, my wife was quiet. I asked her why she looked so bored. She said she wasn't bored, only tired. I snapped back, 'That's the trouble with our marriage. You're always tired. Or rushed. Or something. You're just no fun any more.' She was about to reply, but we had just driven up to her parents' house. We never finished the conversation. When my irritation subsided the next day, I realized what a terrible, and untrue, thing I had said. I really felt ashamed of myself."

Terry worked it out with his wife. And in the long run, the incident had a good outcome. Terry says, "Whenever I'm in a bad mood, I really watch what I say to her."

A negative mood can also lead you to start conversations in ways that are more likely to generate an argument than a productive discussion. Let's say you're not keeping your spending within the budget. You could bring up this topic in various ways. One possibility is, "I'm concerned about the fact that we're spending more money than we have each month. Could we talk about ways to cut back?"

Or if you're in an irritable mood, you might find yourself, like a man in one counseling session, saying, "You've got to stop spending so much of my money. We're never going to make it if you keep acting as if you're married to a wealthy man." The irony of the man's statement is that he was no more controlled in his spending habits than was his wife.

When you're in a negative mood, it's best to talk about the mood itself. In any case, don't blurt out whatever comes to your mind without carefully thinking about what you're going to say and why you're going to say it. A negative mood is an important time to practice reining in the tongue.

"I Want to Connect"

Another reason you may want to share something is that you want to connect with your spouse. As we pointed out in chapter 11, women frequently discuss minor details with their husbands because it's a way to connect, to build intimacy. Men can learn the same lesson. As one husband told us. "I've always tended to be the strong, silent type. My wife tried for years to get me to open up more with her. She said it was important to her and to our relationship that I talk to her. Well, I started to try, mainly to please her. Then I discovered something. It hit me one day. When I would share something with her, it didn't just help her; it helped me too. If I told her something about myself, I felt closer to her. I never realized that when one of us talks to the other, we both feel closer to each other."

Indeed, one of the benefits of sharing is that both spouses feel closer to the other. In terms of building intimacy, it is blessed both to give and to receive thoughts and feelings from the other. If your main motive is to connect with your spouse, therefore, it's generally appropriate to speak. Even so, since we're discussing the sharing of things that could possibly upset or disturb your spouse, you should also answer the rest of the questions before proceeding.

QUESTION 2: WHO WILL BENEFIT?

When you ask yourself who will benefit from what you are about to say, you are likely to answer the question in one of three ways: you will benefit; your spouse will benefit; or you both will benefit.

"I Will Benefit"

In some cases, you may want to share something because it will benefit you in some way. Let's return to the case of Dan and Sharon again. Dan told Sharon of his feelings toward his female student not only because he felt guilty but also because he felt he had something to gain from telling Sharon. He knew that the stress of moving had affected their marriage in a way he didn't like. So another part of his revelation to her was his hope that Sharon would be impressed by how desirable he was. It wasn't just that he found the student attractive; she found him attractive too. Dan wanted Sharon to know that other women found him desirable. That, in turn, would lead her, he hoped, to do something to restore the vitality to their relationship. In essence, he was saying, "It's up to you to make me forget about this other woman."

Unfortunately, Dan came to that insight only after the fact. To be fair, it's very difficult to raise the question of who will benefit and honestly answer that the benefit will primarily be a personal one. Moreover, even if you agree that you will be the primary beneficiary, that doesn't automatically mean you should not share it. But you need to weigh carefully the possible benefits to yourself with the potential harm to your relationship. You may have alternative ways to handle what it is you want to share.

"You Will Benefit"

In some cases you may feel that sharing something will benefit the other person. This is subtle. It sounds *so*

Christian. But it could be a pitfall. If you really believe that your primary purpose is to help your spouse, you need to reflect a bit more. Are you playing the part of God with your spouse? That is, are you trying to shape your spouse in accord with your own will?

For example, a man thinks about saying to his wife, "When we're out in public, you sometimes embarrass me. You tend to get bossy with people. You're not like that with me, but you seem to become a different person when we're with others."

He asks himself why he wants to say it and concludes that he really wants to help his wife. She will be the one who will mainly benefit. After all, he doesn't want people to get turned off by her manner. So he shares his thought with her. In fact, he shared it with her in a counseling session. Matt and Holly were talking about personality issues when Matt made the statement. Holly's response was, "I don't know what to say. I don't feel as if I act any differently when we're with others than when we're together. And I sure don't feel as if I'm a different person when we're with others. When am I so bossy?"

Matt hesitated a moment, then said, "The other night when we were with your sister, you kept telling her what she should do about her son's school problems. You shouldn't tell other people how to run their lives. As I said, you don't do it with me. I'm not complaining about that. You just do it with others."

Holly was still somewhat open-mouthed. "My sister and I have always talked that way to each other," she declared. We continued to explore the matter. Eventually, Matt admitted that what really bothered him was an incident when Holly had been assertive in front of his boss. He was unsettled by it, although it seems to us that Holly's response was not offensive and was entirely appropriate. The boss had invited them to go on his boat some time, and Holly replied, "That's very nice, but I get seasick real easily. Thanks for the offer. Maybe we can do something else together."

Holly is generally an open and assertive woman. Matt fears that she may carry the characteristic too far someday. Although he was saying, "I want to help you," his real purpose was, "I want to help me and safeguard myself against any more embarrassing situations. I will benefit by helping you to be the kind of person I prefer you to be in public."

This isn't to say that "You will benefit" always boils down to "I will benefit." You may truly want to help your spouse in many or most cases. If, for example, Matt had observed Holly offending people by her manner, he could have honestly answered that he was trying to help her.

"We Will Benefit"

A third possibility is that both you and your spouse will benefit. While discussing the personality issue, Matt also said to Holly, "Sometimes when we're having an argument, you just don't listen to me. You interrupt before I can tell you how I feel about something." Holly acknowledged that Matt was correct, and they talked about ways for her to change.

True, Matt will benefit by that change, but so will Holly. As they talked about it, Holly acknowledged that she does the same thing with her friends and business colleagues. "As soon as someone says something, I want to respond. And frequently I do. I don't give them a chance to finish what they're saying. I think that when I do it at work, people take it as an indication of my enthusiasm. At least, they have so far. However, it could get me in trouble someday. I would like to learn to listen to people better. All people. And especially to Matt."

As Holly improves her listening skills, she will benefit, Matt will benefit, and their relationship will benefit. It's important to realize that even though both spouses benefited. Holly was both a little hurt and a bit defensive when Matt first raised the issue of her tendency to interrupt. In fact, she interrupted him to protest that she didn't always interrupt! With a look of chagrin, she admitted her tendency, and the work of changing had begun.

QUESTION 3: WITH WHOM SHOULD I SHARE THIS?

In some cases, after answering the questions of why you want to share and who will benefit, you may decide to keep the matter to yourself. What you had initially felt was important to share was really only a passing feeling or thought that will quietly leave your life.

In other cases, you will decide it's important to you to share your thoughts and feelings. You may feel that the issue is something you must talk over with someone in order to deal with it. If so, then ask yourself who would be the best confidant—your spouse or someone else? If you decide it would be better to talk with someone other than your spouse, whom will it be? You can answer the questions by thinking about two additional questions: Who needs help? and Who can give help?

Who Needs Help?

In the case of Dan and Sharon, who needed help? Clearly, Dan needed it. Sharon needed it only after Dan shared his feelings about his student. Had Dan thought about the situation, he could have reasoned this way: "Who needs help? I need help with my feelings about my student. And I also need help with my marriage. Right now, Sharon is overwhelmed by other problems—loneliness in her new surroundings and a sense of loss because she had to give up her graduate studies."

If Dan had thought that way, he would not have told Sharon about the student. He would have recognized that her self-esteem was at a low ebb and couldn't handle another assault. However, a second issue, the quality of their marriage, needed to be discussed. He could have approached her with something like the following, "Since we moved here, I feel that our marriage has suffered some. I don't feel that we're as close as we were before. I need to talk about it with you and see if you feel the same way. And if you do, we need to figure out what we can do about it. You and our marriage are so important to me."

Sharon would have been delighted to have talked to him about his feelings because it would have given her an opportunity to air her own frustrations. They could have had a productive discussion that would have enriched rather than threatened their marriage.

In the case of Matt and Holly, who needed help? For Holly's supposed bossiness, Matt was the one who needed help. But for her habit of interrupting, she needed help. It was appropriate, therefore, to bring up the habit.

In other words, if the issue is something with which your spouse needs help, you need to raise it. If it is something with which you need help and something that can be distressing to your spouse, you need to consider the possibility of talking with someone else.

Who Can Give Help?

If Dan had reasoned this way, he would have seen that he needed to talk to someone about his student. He needed support in his struggle to deal with his feelings. But he then needed to raise a second question: Who can help me? Obviously, Sharon was not the answer. A friend, a pastor, or a counselor would have been an appropriate person.

Judy illustrates the point in another way. Although she and her husband are both Christians, Judy got emotionally involved with a man at work and came to us while struggling with her feelings. The man wanted to have an affair with her. He took her out to "business" lunches regularly and pressed his case with her. She found him extremely attractive and was having a hard time breaking off the relationship. She made a commitment with us, however, to stop seeing the man and to tell him that she was going to be faithful to her husband.

Judy did not want to tell her husband about her

feelings. But she needed to talk with someone to get the support and help she needed to end the relationship with the man and remain faithful to her husband.

In other words, sometimes you need to talk to someone, but your spouse not only may be hurt by what you have to say but also may be unable to help you in any case. Thus, should a man who experiences lust for other women confess to his wife? A Christian who persistently has such feelings may feel guilty about them. And he may need help to deal with them. But his wife is not likely to be the one to provide the needed help.

Or should a wife who periodically experiences feelings of abhorrence for her husband confess her negative feelings to her husband? Perhaps she is stressed by too many responsibilities and finds herself at times resenting her husband and wishing she were single. If she feels guilty about her feelings, she needs to talk to someone. But her husband is not likely to be the one to help her.

In other words, sometimes it would be better first to go to a pastor, a counselor, or even an understanding and trustworthy friend. If your spouse is likely to be hurt and not likely to be able to give you the help you need, find someone who can help you. Eventually you may want to discuss the issue with your spouse. Or you may not. Talking with someone else first can help you decide that issue also.

QUESTION 4: WILL IT MAKE US FEEL CLOSER TO EACH OTHER?

The final question to ask is, Will sharing this make us feel closer to each other? You may not feel close immediately after talking together, but it's important to assess both the short-term and long-term consequences of sharing.

The Test of Intimacy

A marriage without intimacy is nothing more than two people sharing a house. It is legitimate, therefore, to ask how something might affect your intimacy before sharing it with your spouse. Keep in mind that intimacy develops from such things as openness, sharing, mutual trust, commitment, affection, and security. To assess the possible outcome of sharing something, think about how it might affect those qualities.

Sharing something is itself an intimate act. However, if what you share erodes mutual trust or affection or commitment or security, then your intimacy will clearly suffer. Recall the case of Judy we discussed earlier. Judy came very close to giving in to temptation and having an affair with her colleague. She even agreed to meet him at a motel late one afternoon. She met him there but never went into the room he had rented. The very fact that she had gone there, however, intensified her feelings of guilt.

When we asked Judy whether she would tell her husband about the incident, her response was immediate and firm. No. We wanted her to be certain of her decision, so we explored the matter with her further. Why wasn't she going to tell him? She had already thought it through. "I have a very good marriage now. My husband trusts me. That's one of the things that makes this whole thing really bitter for me. If I tell him, how is he going to trust me in the future? I can tell *you* that he will be able to trust me because I will never allow myself to get in that kind of situation again. But if I were in his shoes, I know I would have a hard time with the trust.

"I also know he would be very hurt. It tears me up just to think of the hurt on his face. I won't do that to him. I won't do that to *us.*"

In her assessment, Judy was applying the test of intimacy to her decision. She specifically mentioned trust. And in saying "I won't do that to *us,*" she recognized that the quality of her relationship would be diminished.

We did not let the matter rest there. We posed a hypothetical situation. "You say that it pains you to know that you have violated his trust. How are you going to handle it if sometime in the future something like this would happen? Let's say you are with some friends, and the issue of faithless marriages comes up. Your husband puts his arm around you and says how grateful he is that the two of you have always had complete trust in each other. How will you handle that?"

Judy smiled, then said. "You don't know my husband. He doesn't talk like that. But, okay. Let's say it did happen. I can handle it. In fact, I can do better than that. Because right now, I don't feel very secure about my marriage. At times I'm afraid that he has sensed my feelings. I haven't been as warm and loving toward him as I used to be. But I'm going to make it up to him. And if he said that, it would make me feel very grateful and secure again."

Using the test of intimacy, then, Judy made her decision not to tell her husband. She told us that at times she was on the verge of breaking down and telling him everything. Yet she kept a rein on her tongue, not simply to save face, but for the sake of her husband and their relationship.

Periodic Assessments

In addition to raising the question of intimacy before sharing something with your spouse, it's also helpful periodically to ask yourself after an open discussion whether the talking made you feel closer to each other. We have focused on the question of whether to tell your spouse something that might hurt or distress him or her. And so far, we have mainly discussed telling your spouse something that you have thought or felt or done.

But you may also want to consider not talking together about certain topics. The topics don't involve anything like an act of betrayal or a hurtful criticism. They are simply topics about which you disagree.

For example, we got to know a couple who carried on stimulating conversations with us about a variety of topics. One evening, we began to talk about how each of them viewed the role of women in our society. They looked at each other, then the husband told us that they simply didn't discuss the topic because they disagreed. They had talked about it a number of times, realized afterward that it always left them feeling alienated from each other, and decided to avoid it. Each had strong feelings and opinions about the topic. Yet they opted against talking with each other every time their feelings were stirred by an incident or a news item. They valued their marriage more than their differing opinions. They realized that if talking about something doesn't make you feel closer afterward, it may be best to avoid the topic. The whole point of openness and honesty, after all, is not to provide you with a personal resident therapist but rather to enhance your experience of intimacy.

The point is, you don't have to work out all your disagreements. If you disagree over such things as how to discipline the children or how to budget your money, you need to come to some kind of mutually satisfactory resolution. But you don't have to iron out your differences over such things as which political party to support or what color the new church carpet should be. If those differences cause friction between you whenever you discuss them, it's best to acknowledge your differences and avoid the discussions.

We know many happy couples who are divided on external matters like politics. What they have learned is that their differing ideas on externals are not as important as their relationship. As a husband of twenty-seven years put it, "When we were married, my wife was a strong Democrat and I was a strong Republican. We spent the first ten years of our marriage trying to convert each other. Every election, we would argue and argue about issues and candidates. We would get mad at each other and stay mad—at least off and on—until the election was over.

"Guess what happened after ten years? I was still a strong Republican and my wife was still a strong Democrat. But we realized that we had kind of been shooting ourselves in the foot. What was the point? We agreed that from then on, we would just accept each other's political views but not talk about them. We know how the other is going to vote, but it doesn't matter any more. Our marriage is more important than our politics. For ten years, politics was like crabgrass in our marriage. Since we stopped talking about it, our marriage has been more rewarding than ever."

We heard a similar story from a woman who said that an incident put a strain on her marriage for a year. "I work with a guy who tends to touch people when he talks to them. When my husband and I were grocery shopping one day, we saw this guy in the store. We talked a while. Since we were in a hurry, my husband excused himself and finished the shopping while I kept talking.

"When we got into the car, I could tell my husband was angry. I thought it was because we were running late for a meeting with some friends. I told him to not worry because our friends were usually late anyway. He said that wasn't what was bothering him. Then he accused me of flirting with my friend from work. He said we each had our hands all over the other. I told him my friend does that with everyone and that I didn't recall putting my hands on him.

"Would you believe that we disagreed over that for a year? My husband kept insisting that it was flirting. And I kept insisting that it was totally innocent. That was six years ago. If you raised it today, I'm sure he would still say it was flirting. And I still know it was innocent."

How did these two spouses get beyond it? They agreed that their perspectives differed and decided not to talk about it anymore. We pointed out in an earlier chapter that to "agree to disagree" can be dishonest if it means that you are hiding some of your true feelings. But if you have each expressed yourselves fully and still differ, it may be best to agree not only to disagree but also to refrain from discussing the matter any more.

What it all boils down to is this: Marital intimacy is one of the precious gifts that God has given us. We must cherish it, guard it, and nurture it. And remember that a bridled tongue that speaks the truth in love—rather than transparent honesty about every thought and feeling we have or the insistence that we must agree on everything—is the surest route to a relationship that is both lasting and enriching.

CHAPTER 14

Allen and Betsy: An Honest Couple

We would like you to meet an honest couple, although they weren't always that way. We want you to meet Allen and Betsy for four reasons. First, they illustrate some of the principles we have discussed in this book. Second, they show the rewards of building an honest relationship. Third, they demonstrate how dishonesty can flourish even when it is not intentional and neither spouse is aware of it. Fourth, their experience dramatizes the importance of one final principle that underlies all else that we have written in this book: *Assumptions are the deadly enemy of an honest relationship.*

Allen and Betsy, both in their forties, met at church, where they attended a college Bible study group. It was not a love-at-first-sight meeting. Rather, they gradually got to know each other over several months' time and increasingly found that they had many interests and aspirations in common. They both enjoyed tennis, swimming, and movies. Both were active in church. Both planned to be high-school teachers, and eventually each wanted a family. As they discussed their childhood experiences, they also realized that their families were similar in very important ways.

They knew each other for two years before they started dating. By that time, they were already good friends. The minister who officiated at their wedding said to them, "You have an excellent foundation for a lasting and happy marriage. You are so much alike and enjoy each other so much that I can't imagine your marriage not lasting."

In spite of this strong foundation, however, Allen and Betsy's marriage almost didn't survive. For the first three years, everything went well. They taught at the same school: Betsy taught psychology and did some counseling; Allen taught math and coached the boys' basketball team. Then Betsy got pregnant. If babies are a blessing, Allen and Betsy were doubly blessed. They had twins.

Allen and Betsy had agreed from the start that she would stop working until their children were in school. Betsy left her job and became a full-time mother and homemaker.

Soon after the twins were born, problems began to develop in their marriage. At first the problems were barely noticeable. It was just little things, like Allen spending more time at school meetings, extra-curricular activities, and teaching responsibilities—all of which left him little time to help with the babies. As a result, Betsy was exhausted most of the time. When Allen wanted to make love, she often resisted because she was so tired.

At first each spouse was understanding of the other. But Allen became increasingly involved with the school, and Betsy became increasingly absorbed with motherhood. Love making stopped altogether. Communication degenerated into trivial conversations or arguments.

They reached a low point one day when Betsy asked Allen if he could stay home that evening and take care of the twins while she got caught up on the rest she had lost spending long night hours with two sick babies. Allen said no. When Betsy asked him why he couldn't help her, he said he had a parents' meeting with the basketball team. Betsy lost control and started shouting at him. Allen shouted back and stormed out of the house.

How had it come to this? Betsy recalls, "It was a low point in our marriage. It felt as if Allen had already divorced me. He had distanced himself so far from the children and me that I hardly saw him as my husband anymore. He didn't care that I was exhausted three-fourths of the time. He never offered to help me. He never volunteered to take care of the kids. He just did whatever he wanted to do. I needed help. I needed a husband who would at least support me and appreciate what I was doing. Allen didn't give me anything. I was ready to call it quits."

Allen saw things a bit differently. "I felt Betsy had lost interest in me and our marriage. After the twins were born, she got so caught up in them that she didn't pay any attention to me. So I got involved in more things at work. If I tried to get close to her, she would just remind me of how tired she was. She didn't want my affection or love. She wanted me to be a housekeeper and baby-sitter. If I resisted, she got mad. It never occurred to her that I was tired too. My work is demanding even when I don't take on the extra stuff. I was fed up and ready to walk."

Note that both Allen and Betsy were *making assumptions* about the other. Betsy said that Allen already had divorced himself from her and the children; Allen said Betsy had rejected his affection and love. Allen said that Betsy only wanted a housekeeper and baby-sitter; Betsy said that she needed his support and appreciation as well as his help in caring for the house and children.

In other words, both Allen and Betsy were reacting to the other person on the basis of erroneous assumptions. Neither person was honest with the other about his or her true feelings and needs because each assumed the other wasn't interested. And whatever either of them did, the other spouse interpreted the actions as confirmation of the erroneous assumptions.

For instance, when Allen once asked Betsy if she wanted him to hold one of the twins while she took care of the other, she assumed he was only trying to soften her up so that he could ask her to have sex later that night. She curtly said no. However, Allen was only trying to break through the hostility that separated them. Her reactions confirmed his assumption that Betsy was interested only in the children and not in him.

Similarly, when Betsy once suggested to Allen that she put the twins to bed so that they could have some time to talk together, Allen assumed she wanted to complain again about her exhaustion and to insist that he would do more work around the house. Not wanting to get into that argument again, he said he had to leave for a meeting and that they would have to talk another time. Actually, Betsy was trying to see if they could stop the downward spiral of their relationship and begin to rebuild it. His reaction only confirmed her assumption that he didn't care about her.

How did they work their way out of the situation? In this case, they did it themselves. Betsy had some training in therapeutic techniques, which she used when she counseled her students. The breakthrough came one day when the twins were asleep and Betsy had some quiet time to think about the misery in their marriage. Suddenly the thought occurred to her, "What would I tell one of my students if she came to me and told me her parents were acting the way Allen and I are?"

Betsy realized that she and Allen had been breaking all the rules and principles she would have suggested to others. She had a counseling session with herself, telling herself about her problems and then responding to herself as a counselor. With a prayer for added strength, she chose a plan of action.

That night Allen came home to a candlelight dinner. One of his favorite meals—lasagna—was on the table. He was startled. Not knowing what to say, he said nothing about the dinner. He talked about his day at school. He asked Betsy about her day with the twins. "By the way," he said, looking around, "where are they? Asleep already?" Betsy told him they were at the neighbors' house.

They chatted a bit more, then Allen said to her in a questioning voice, "I just don't know what to say. I do hope this isn't some sort of last meal." Clearly he was wondering about the change, but he was skeptical.

Betsy felt the anger rise in her, but she quenched it. "Don't you remember how much you loved this when we were first married?" she asked. He nodded. "I just thought it would be a good way to start recapturing those days."

Betsy's voice quivered. For all she knew at that point, Allen might have responded by telling her that he had no interest in recapturing those days. But Allen just stared at her for a moment, and then his eyes filled with tears.

That night was a breakthrough. But it wasn't a revolution. Allen and Betsy still had to work through many troublesome days. It had taken them a long time to reach the low point in their marriage, so it was not likely that they would totally transform their relationship in a few weeks. But they certainly redirected it. And one of the things that helped keep the new direction was Betsy's determination to have an honest relationship. "On that pivotal afternoon when I finally faced the problems in our marriage at close range, I began to think of all those case studies I had read about couples in trouble, about how many of them did just what Allen and I were doing—assuming the worst about each other without making the effort to find out what the other was really thinking and feeling."

The candlelight dinner made it clear to both Allen and Betsy that they had been misinterpreting the other. Neither of them wanted the marriage to end. Both were miserable about the way their relationship had deteriorated. Betsy suggested that they work out a plan of action to rebuild their marriage. Their list of things to do included spending more time together, taking more care to help each other, and avoiding assumptions about the other's words and actions.

It didn't take them long to realize that their list was too general. They needed to get more specific. So they planned a weekly date night, leaving the twins with the neighbors or a baby-sitter. Helping each other meant that each would have to be honest about the extent of weariness each expressed.

"No more pretending to be more tired than we really are in order to rub it in or get the advantage," Betsy said. Each would at times have to take on a little extra work to relieve the other.

Finally, avoiding assumptions meant that each of them would be careful both to ask how the other was feeling as well as to express his or her own feelings. "In other words," Allen noted, "I couldn't come home anymore and dare Betsy to figure out why I felt as I did. I had to let her know how I felt and why I thought I felt that way."

The upshot is that now, ten years later, Allen and Betsy are happier than they've ever been before. It isn't that they never argue. It isn't that they have no harrowing days—the twins assure a steady supply of those. And it isn't that they share every thought or feeling with each other.

Rather, the happiness comes from a sense that they can trust each other to be honest. They don't have to play guessing games with each other. They don't have to fret because of erroneous assumptions. They don't have to pry any secrets from each other. They trust each other to be frank about thoughts and feelings. They know that if either of them lapses, the other will bring him or her back to honesty by asking candid questions. They have worked hard to create an honest relationship.

Betsy and Allen daily give thanks to God for each other, and they rejoice in the life they have built together. Their marriage is not trouble-free. Like everyone else, they sometimes still struggle, but their efforts have borne fruit. They have built an honest and fulfilling marriage.